Heart Circles

How Sitting in Circle Can Transform Your World

by Tej Steiner

INTERACTIVE MEDIA PUBLISHING

Heart Circles

How Sitting in Circle
Can Transform Your World

By Tej Steiner

First Edition
Copyright © 2006 Tej Steiner
Artwork Copyright © 2006 Andre' Brighteyes, Living Light Creations

To order additional copies of this book, go to www.heartcircle.com or contact the publisher.

ISBN: 0-9744391-8-5
Published in the U.S. by:
Interactive Media Publishing
PO Box 1407, 111 East. 1st St
Phoenix, OR 97535
(541) 535-5552

Dedication

To Caryn

Heart Circle Participants

"Group for me was undoubtedly the best healing and growth experience of my life... Bar None! Nothing on this earth has ever provided me the safety, confidentiality, and permission to be myself that, weekly, I found sitting in Circle." Bernie Ahearn, Detroit, MI

"To be given a space to share without fear is one of the greatest gifts of the Heart Circle format. It provides an opportunity to truly understand what it means to be honest." Jack Cornflower, Ashland, OR

"My Heart Circle is my healthy chosen family. Being with my Heart Circle feels like womb comfort. Sometimes, I feel in love with all Life, every moment tasting like nectar. Sometimes I'm contracted, insecurity or paranoia interfering with my interior sense of peace & calm. Either way, I always show up honestly and I know that I am loved. Our commitment to honesty and expressing what we want always ensures a very creative and rich experience." Shyama Harris, Sebastapol, CA

"I feel deeply grateful for our Circle, for the presence of Love, and holding space for each other. It is a potent 'transformer' for myself as part of our Circle, our community, and our world community." Johti Rundel, Ashland, OR

"Tej has a different lens on human relationships and growth from

anyone I've known. It's quite remarkable and wonderfully healing."
Jeff Golden, Ashland, OR

"*From my experience there's a kind of magical energy that happens in Heart Circles; the kind of energy that can change a person's life and help manifest their heart's desire. I believe the world will change as more people make the commitment to come into Circle.*"
Dave Cobb, Sterling Heights, MI

"*I have found this container to be life-changing from several points: spending conscious time focused on my feelings and how my body is holding my feelings, holding space for others doing the same, being aware of how rare and important this is. Being in Heart Circle has enriched my life.*" Joanna Gabriel, Ashland, OR

"*The Circle created a safe place to experiment with new behaviors and receive loving feedback that supported my growth and changes.*"
Lenn Snyder, Phoenix, OR

"*I have worked with many masters in the area of group dynamics and facilitation, none more intuitive and articulate than Tej Steiner. His work is truly transformational and must be experienced if you want to understand the power of gathering in circles. He creates strong connections between people, using the simple, but powerful inquiry, 'What do you want?' Through Circle, I have experienced profound joy, clarity, inspiration, and deep healing.*" Rachael Kennedy, Ashland, OR

Contents

Heart Circle Definition

Heart Circles are small, self-facilitated support groups for people wanting to become more creative, joyful, intuitive, heart-directed and responsive to the uncertain times in which we live. When people sit in Circle with each other to explore what they truly want to create in their lives and world, they connect quickly and deeply.

A new kind of community can emerge from this connection. The community holds space for individuals to live life directed by what they truly want instead of what they should or shouldn't do. Those individuals then offer back to the community the vitality and creativity of their passion and clarity of purpose. This strengthens the community which in turn creates an even more nurturing environment for the individuals within it. And on and on it goes.

These kinds of self-organized Circles are not only joyful and effective, but they also may be crucial in building sustainable communities to take us safely through this period of global transition from competition and fear to cooperation and love.

A Time For
Heart Circles

A Time For Heart Circles

Our species is at an evolutionary crossroads: we are moving out of individual survival and collective competition into individual happiness and collective cooperation.

How would your life change if you found out how to deliberately create joy or inner peace whenever you really wanted to? This would mean that whenever you were in a bad mood, you would know how to quickly change into a good mood or that whenever you were feeling depressed, angry or unworthy, you could move into feeling balanced, relaxed, and confident. If you knew how to do this and got quite good at it, how would it affect your primary partnership or your effectiveness as a parent or your ability to succeed in anything that you wanted to do?

If most of the people in the world knew how to create their own happiness, regardless of their circumstances, how would the world change from the way it is now?

We are now moving into a new era in which this is exactly what is beginning to happen, collectively. Just as the last one hundred years have brought us amazing changes in technology and information sharing, the next one hundred years are going to bring us equally amazing changes in our ability to deliberately move into personal joy and connection with all of life.

This is not a utopian dream for the millions of culturally creative people on the planet today who are already engaged in this transformational process and who are beginning to understand how it works in their own lives.

You are probably one of these pioneers, if you are reading this book. We have read many of the same books about consciousness. We try to eat foods that aren't poisoned. We work in jobs that actually produce something of value. We are sickened by ecological abuse and by war. Most of us are more spiritual than religious and many of us are social activists.

Knowing how to deliberately move from suffering will greatly affect human history. It is what we have been evolving toward, as a species, throughout time. Every human being is hardwired, first to survive and then to move from suffering to personal fulfillment and ever-expanding creativity. Until now, we have collectively been in 'survival mode,' as a species. But technology has made survival less of a personal daily issue, at the same time that our brains and consciousness have been evolving. We are at a crossroads at which there is now room for a species-wide response to life from our higher intelligence cerebral cortexes, rather than the lower reactive brain centers .

Much of the insanity that we are seeing in the world right now can be traced to the fact that during this period of revolutionary transition to a higher functioning, co-operative, heart-directed paradigm, our advanced technologies and our political and financial organizations are still in the hands of people who are operating out of a fear-based survival paradigm. Insensitivity to nature, a reversion to religious fundamentalism, a pandemic of corporate-government corruption, absurd levels of consumption and destructive lifestyles are the creations of disconnected, unhappy people. Whoever heard of a joyful criminal?

But this technology-driven mass culture that we have created is, itself, a transitional stage in our human cultural history. We know it is transitional because it simply is not sustainable. It must evolve into something else since what we are doing now is collapsing the ecological and social systems that sustain life. Many of our collective, political choices around the world mimic the absurdity of those investors who are today building billion dollar casinos in the desert where the water's running out. Those of us who have deliberately left this mass culture paradigm can only scratch our heads and ask, "What's up with that?"

As our mass culture evolves into something more sensible and sustainable, it may cause tremendous destruction on its way out. It may come with extreme violence and immense suffering, as we can see already occurring in many parts of the world in which contaminated environments and economic stagnation reflect larger patterns of non-sustainable policies. There is no one to blame here, only rampant disconnection from our collective inner wisdom.

From this evolutionary point of view, all of us, as individual human beings, may have the exact same life purpose and imperatives in terms of moving into this higher, co-operative, joyful functioning which gives us access to what has before been 'hidden behind the veil':

- *It includes tapping into our vast creative potential that was, before, accessed only by the visionary genius.*

- *It includes being freed from any sense of shameful unworthiness that was, before, accessed only by the fully loved child.*

- *It includes our directly experiencing the connection which we have to 'Everything Else' that was, before, accessed only by the mystical saint or sage.*

Collectively, we have greater access to the choice of living in creative joy, consciously.

So, this brings us full circle: How would life change if you found out how to create joy or inner peace whenever you wanted to?

There are certain insights or principles which we must understand and to which we must adhere in order to move from suffering to joy.

There are several preliminary understandings that we must absorb in terms of how to do this. First and foremost, we must feel that it's *possible* to create joy intentionally in order for us to be able to do so. This is an 'entry level' requirement.

Also, many of us have experienced the understanding that there is no fixed recipe for creating happiness, such as 'Pray at noon and eat nine bananas every day!' It doesn't work like that, even though many sales oriented teachers have taught that it does.

While there is no 'one way,' there are certain fixed laws or principles that we must understand and adhere to in order to move from suffering to joy. According to the Abraham/Hicks teachings, foremost of these principles is the 'Law of Attraction,' which says that what we give our attention to is what we attract to us. It means that our individual intelligence is in a constant interactive process with the Universal Intelligence and that what we focus on in our moment-to-moment lives is what we manifest in our lives. If we give our attention to what we fear, we attract to us what we fear. If we give our attention to what we love, then we attract to us what we love.

The practical implications of this are vast. What if the key to being deliberately happy is learning how to keep our moment-to-moment attention on what makes us happy? This would mean that we have an internal guidance system which we can use, if we are willing to follow it. We have a chance to ask, in every moment, what it is that we truly want, knowing that life will begin organizing itself around those wants the moment we allow ourselves to feel them fully.

The small support group format provides a perfect environment in which to explore our lives from this evolutionary perspective.

As a life-long student of how to consciously move into joy, I have been fascinated by one particular tool that I knew was extraordinarily effective: the small circle support group. Sitting in Circle with a handful of others can be highly intimate and reflective. It is democratic by nature. It can provide a safe, cozy container in which people learn to trust and receive from each other inspiration, friendship, reassurance, and honest communication around whatever purpose the circle is formed.

Through AA and other 'addiction support groups,' millions of people have been given a solid base from which to face their deepest fears. There are also 'emotional processing groups,' developed during the past 40 years, in which millions of other people have broken out of the emotional repression that has been passed down through generations. At the same time, men's and women's groups have formed, allowing people the safety in which to explore the uncharted waters of the deep feminine and deep masculine. Today, there are support groups for anything that requires courage and community and collective wisdom: for grieving, dying, healing, and praying and for being consciously sexual, single, married, divorced, or widowed.

I started out studying small-group dynamics in Toronto, Canada with Dr. Ross Laing a teacher who is a brilliant facilitator of emotional processing and spiritual healing. This led to my facilitating men's and couple's groups for twenty years, during which time I was a part of or facilitated over four thousand small group circles. Throughout this time, I was most fascinated by the question of how small support groups could sustain people in terms of deliberately moving from suffering to joy.

It was this root question that brought me to the profound realization that all of these support groups, with all of the good that they do, can become even more effective if they add one essential element: the deliberate inquiry into what people truly want in their lives. Without this direct, primary question of 'What do you want?' there is a tendency to remain mired in whatever 'problem' the group was formed to resolve. For example, in some addiction recovery groups, people continue defining themselves in relationship to their addictions, well past their actual recovery. In emotional processing groups, the focus is often concentrated on uncovering deeper and deeper negative emotions, despite the fact that the more they focus on emotional clearing, the more emotions they will have to clear.

In 1989, I started forming small circle groups in which the primary focus was on creating joy by providing an environment in which people could reflect on and discuss what brings them happiness. I learned that, with this focus, people could more easily move from what they feared and what wasn't working for them to what they loved and wanted. And using the universal principle of 'ask and it shall be given,' I watched how people's lives changed as they began to attract to themselves not just 'things' that they wanted, but what they wanted to become. Everyone wants to be happy, empowered, peaceful and passionate. By feeling the innate longing to be so begins the fulfillment process that makes it so.

I also found that when people are communicating what they are honestly feeling and what they truly want, it brings them close together very quickly. Trust is created as Circle members invite each other into deeper honesty. The Circle becomes a place in which people encircle each other's hearts and, from this intimate sharing, community is born.

In 2001, I started calling these small groups 'Heart Circles.' They are designed for people to explore their capacity to intentionally live in joy while, at the same time, creating community with those with whom they are in Circle.

The purpose of this book is to show you how to create your own self-organized and self-facilitated Heart Circle.

While Heart Circles are elegantly simple in design, they are also quite specific in terms of how they are meant to function. The purpose of this book is to describe the function of Heart Circles. I want to demonstrate clearly and precisely how anyone or any organization can self-organize and facilitate a Heart Circle, using this book as a tool. And, as a tool, the book will lay out a template for how a Heart Circle functions and around what ideas it is developed. I will begin with the benefits of being in a Heart Circle, and continue with its theory and structure, and how to form, implement, and sustain one of these life altering groups.

What I offer in this book has been a collaborative process with the thousands of people with whom I have sat in Circle. My hope is that this Heart Circle concept and process will continue to be a collaborative experiment between all of you who are motivated to participate in a Heart Circle of your own. In this way, the Heart Circle design will continue to grow dynamically as an ever new and more effective 'social invention.'

One last insight in this Heart Circles introduction: at this stage of our evolutionary history, we must actually learn how to deliberately create joy through constant trial and error. We are just 'babes' in this evolutionary process of coming into our hearts. This will change in the future when the pathways to joy are better understood scientifically or through 'collective wisdom.' Until then, we are all in this together, trying to find our way at dawn.

So, I invite you to enjoy the process of reading this book and sharing its possibilities with others. Whether you agree or disagree with what's written is not as important as your awareness of what arises within you as you read it. Being a passionate witness to your internal process is itself valuable and it draws to you courageous people who are doing the same. I believe that the times in which we live ask for this kind of heart exploration and awaits our response.

The Ideas
Surrounding
Heart Circles

The Ideas Surrounding Heart Circles

Most of us had little personal support in deliberately creating happiness and connection as we grew up in our society.

How do we deliberately move from feeling unhappy, depressed, hopeless, bored, bad, angry, confused, and unworthy to feeling happy, confident, creative, energized, grateful, good, peaceful, connected, and joyful?   And why wouldn't this be the most important question in our own personal lives and the question around which our entire culture organizes itself?

If we take a quick look around us, we see that we are not being particularly successful in answering these questions; there is an immense amount of suffering in our world. Many of us are medicated, obese, addicted, imprisoned, in meaningless jobs, in poverty, depressed, lonely, angry, bored, and sick or and at war in some way with something. And as for our basic social structures in society, are they providing meaningful guidance in terms of how to deliberately sustain happiness?

In the basic family unit, did the topic regularly come up at the dinner table as you were growing up; did your father and mother ask how you were doing in your daily quest to feel more confident, worthy, brilliantly bright and happy?

In school did one of your teachers ever close the textbook and say, "Today we are going to talk about who in the class is happy and who is not and then explore ways for all of you to make your life more joyful and fulfilling"?

In the world of politics, did you ever heard a politician say, "This is the most powerful country in the world, but that does not make us the happiest people in the world. I am dedicated to working with all of you to make us a joyful nation"?

Did you ever have a minister or priest say, "God is joy and, therefore, being joyful is being one with God. Let's increase our joy together by following what brings us joy"? End of sermon.

Of course, it can be argued that there is an underlying

26

'assumption' that happiness is what all of us want. Parents, obviously, want their children to be happy. People get married so that they will be happy. Schools educate students so they will be happy later. Governments govern to make at least the majority happy. And religions offer prescribed beliefs and practices that will lead to happiness.

But, if we were all pursuing happiness with this clear intention, why would this assumption be so unspoken? If a company sells computers, it would not be an unspoken assumption that this is what it sells. It would be spoken every day, every hour: "We sell computers. Do you want to buy one?" And the manager of a baseball team wouldn't manage with an unspoken assumption that his or her team wants to win. He wouldn't say, "We all know how much we want to win this game today, so let's not talk about it."

Therefore, if moving from suffering to joy in life was our first priority, why wouldn't this be clear to everyone? And, if everyone is clear about this, why are so many millions of us in so much pain?

One answer to this question is that creating our own happiness is not our mainstream culture's first priority because it's operating out of an old paradigm that says happiness is circumstantial and out of our direct control: we are happy only to the extent that favorable circumstances make us happy.

But this is rapidly changing. A new paradigm is alive in our world in which people are acknowledging that there are basic principles governing being happy, and that understanding and honoring these principles does lead to greater joy, gratitude, creativity, and happiness.

Increasing numbers of teachers are introducing this paradigm into our culture. Esther and Jerry Hicks and their 'Abraham' teachings are some of the clearest voices doing this. The following segment is a synopsis of this new paradigm.

Heart Circles works with principles or insights that provide a foundation for deliberately creating joy. Here are eight of those insights.

If creating our own happiness could be done in eight or ten easy steps, someone, by now, would have named those steps, and we all would have merrily followed them and lived happily ever after. And, even if it were about following steps, there would be thousands of steps to follow, making life laboriously proscriptive and complicated. Rather than steps, it is more about exploring certain principles that govern our being happy than about seeking to apply these principles to our daily lives.

In Heart Circles, no one says that you have to believe in these principles. Instead, you are invited to explore them so that you can experience for yourself what is true. For example, when learning how to drive a car, believing that the brake pedal stops the car comes from experiencing that it does; your belief is based upon your experience.

Heart Circles are designed to create an environment in which you can explore the following principles experientially rather than intellectually:

One:
Everyone moves back and forth between happiness and unhappiness continuously, between feeling high and feeling low, between feeling good and feeling bad.

This can be symbolized with a simple line continuum, having arrows at both ends and a small line down the middle:

On one side of the middle line is happiness in ever increasing degrees and on the other is unhappiness in ever increasing degrees. The words "happiness" and "unhappiness" are interchangeable with other opposites: "connection" and "disconnection," "joy" and "suffering." "high energy states" and "low energy states," etc.

In this moment or in any moment of your life, you can plot on that line what degree of happiness or unhappiness you happen to be feeling. Said another way, you can determine whether you are vibrating at higher energy states that manifest as joy, vitality, creativity, passion, and contentment or at lower frequencies which manifest as struggle, loneliness, shame, alienation, anger, and pain.

You do this by 'observing' or 'becoming aware of' what you are feeling in any given moment. You develop your capacity to 'witness' your own emotional state.

Right now, you could be feeling deep despair or alienation and be in low frequency:

Or you could be feeling ecstatically happy and be in high frequency:

Or you can be somewhere in the middle, on either side of the line. If you feel neutral, neither happy nor unhappy, you would plot that on the left hand side of the line. On the right, you would feel vaguely happy and content, but definitely not ecstatic:

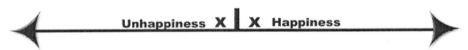

Most people continuously travel back and forth on this line, as their feeling state fluctuates from moment to moment, day to day, month to month, or year to year..

You could also be living a predominately unhappy life, staying on the left hand side of the line, not really knowing what it's like to be happy for more than a moment or two at a time.

Or you can be living a predominantly happy life, staying on the left hand side of the line, and visiting the right side of the line only occasionally.

Most people live somewhere in the middle, going back and forth over the line many times in any given day, week, month, or year..

To show this, we can simply turn the line into a time/ feeling graph, and show how at various times, we fluc- tuate on this feeling state continuum.

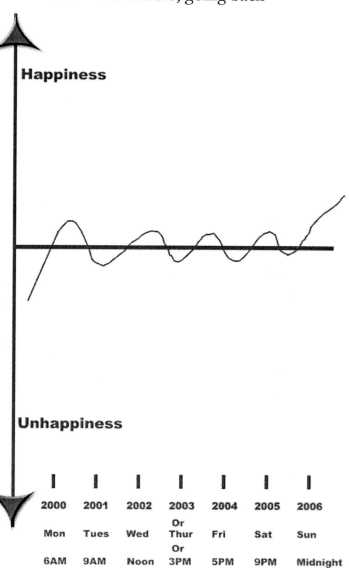

Happiness

Unhappiness

2000	2001	2002	2003 Or	2004	2005	2006
Mon	Tues	Wed	Thur Or	Fri	Sat	Sun
6AM	9AM	Noon	3PM	5PM	9PM	Midnight

So, borrowing directly from the Hicks/Abraham teachings, we can now fill in the different feeling states that are associated with happiness and unhappiness:

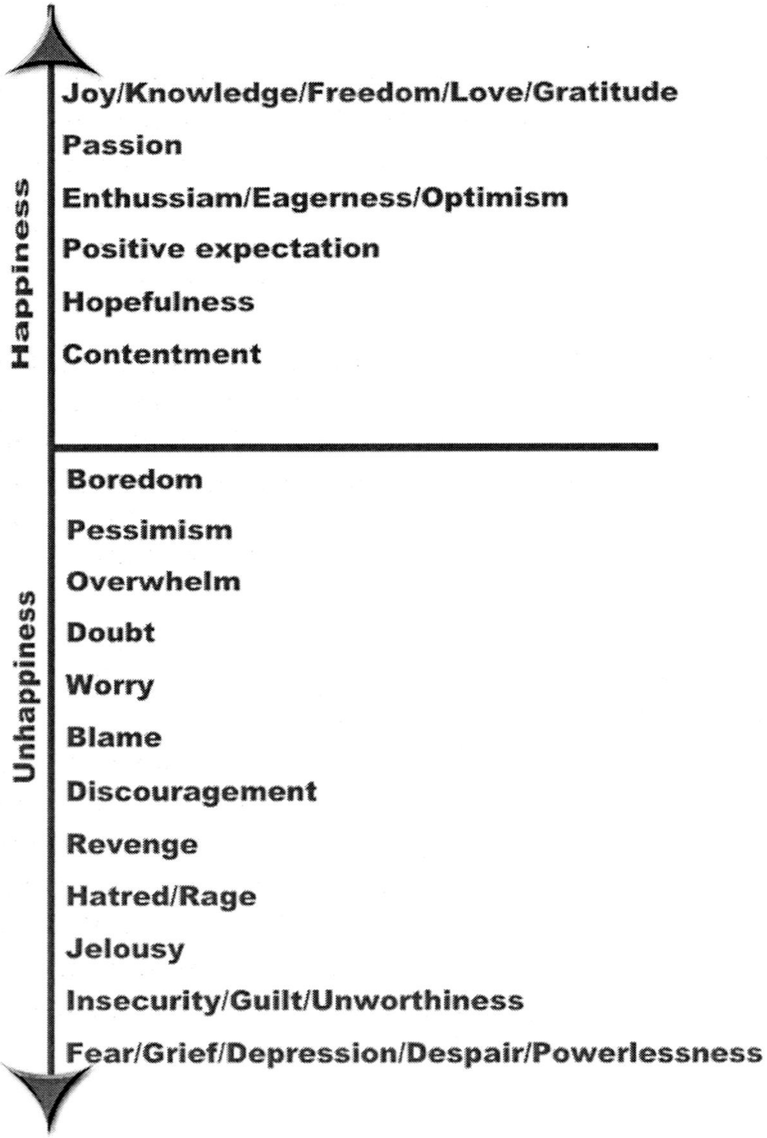

Happiness

Joy/Knowledge/Freedom/Love/Gratitude

Passion

Enthussiam/Eagerness/Optimism

Positive expectation

Hopefulness

Contentment

Unhappiness

Boredom

Pessimism

Overwhelm

Doubt

Worry

Blame

Discouragement

Revenge

Hatred/Rage

Jelousy

Insecurity/Guilt/Unworthiness

Fear/Grief/Depression/Despair/Powerlessness

Two:
There is a desire, whether conscious or unconscious, in everyone to move out of pain and suffering and into happiness and joy.

This basic desire for happiness is hardwired into everyone: we all move toward what feels 'good,' and away from what feels 'bad.' Joy feels good and suffering doesn't. We all want to be happy, regardless of whether or not we understand how to be so. In this way, we all share the same purpose in life: to experience this happiness.

If we think that 'loving others' or 'making the world better' is the purpose of life, then we are confusing the means with the ends: loving others feels good and leads to personal happiness, while hating others doesn't feel good, and leads to unhappiness. Passionately offering our gifts to the world feels wonderful, while withholding our gifts does not.

Also, we can't truly give to others if we are in the lower energy states of feeling depressed, unworthy, and joyless because what we ultimately give others is our love, joy, and energy. Therefore, our motivations for serving others can differ: serving to cover up our own pain, serving as a way to come out of our pain, or serving as a pure expression of the love that we feel for others. But, even with these three different motivations, serving others is still intrinsically linked to our own longing to be in joy and in a higher energy state.

Three:
There is a pivotal 'awakening' when we realize that we can actually choose to be in these higher energy states of joy, connection, and creativity.

Once we are consciously aware of our purpose to live in joy and the higher energy states of creativity, love, and well being, the obvious question becomes how do we do this? How do we raise our own energy state so that we are experiencing joy more often, and can we do this deliberately?

These two questions are central to all religions, spiritual practices, psychotherapeutic processes, and healing techniques. For example, to experience greater joy and connection we can:

Follow certain religious traditions: Christianity, Buddhism, Judaism, Islam, etc.

Make certain lifestyle choices: eating well, living in beautiful environments, choosing meaningful work, etc.

Explore personal and transpersonal psychology: releasing birth shock, parental interjects, negative thought patterns, and other subconscious little critters, etc.

Find ways to express life through art: dancing, painting, singing, etc.

Practicing any of the hundreds of mind-body therapeutic

disciplines: tai chi, chi gong, yoga, etc.

And then, there is simply doing whatever we do more consciously: breathing, parenting, working, listening, serving others, etc.

Four:
The 'ultimate' practice for being in joy is to feel and then choose that which brings us joy. ('Joy' can be replaced with other words: peace, contentment, being in the moment, love, etc.)

All of the practices listed above have one thing in common: we engage in them because we want the joy, peace, wisdom, or love that comes from that engagement. Whether it's 'being in the moment,' playing basketball in the zone, or singing 'Glory Hallelujah' on the corner of 5th and Main, it is all to fulfill our purpose in moving from feeling bad to feeling good, from lower energetic states to higher, from disconnection to connection.

But, what if we did EVERYTHING to fulfill this purpose? What if we chose, a thousand times a day, to engage in that which brings us joy over that which doesn't? To be more loving, we would feel and follow what we love. We would follow what our hearts want or 'follow our bliss,' as Joseph Campbell says.

Becoming more sensitive to what we truly want includes:

- What do I want to feel? I am feeling angry right now. I want to feel this anger long enough to find out why I am angry and then move into feeling more compassionate or peaceful.

- What do I want to think? I'm thinking that I will never complete this project successfully. I want to think that I'm right on schedule and that I will complete it easily.

- What do I want to have? I want to generate more income so that I can easily pay off all my debts.

- What do I want to do? I really want to have lunch with my two closest friends next Wednesday.

These questions can be asked in relation to the present moment or to the future. What do you want right now and what do you want in the coming months? This is not an intellectual exercise; it is an experiential practice. What we truly want and are passionate about is a 'felt sense' that can be enhanced so that we become clearer and clearer as to what we really want in any given moment.

 *__Five:__*
__There is a direct relationship between what we want and what we receive.__

In the Abraham/Hicks teachings, the 'Law of Attraction' states that we attract to us what we give our attention to. This means that the Universe is responsive to what we are thinking, feeling, wanting, and doing. Life itself organizes itself around what we want and are ready to receive. We are intelligent, energetic beings, sending out continuous, vibrational signals to the Universe in the form of our desires, beliefs, and intentions, and these signals are matched perfectly with what is given back to us.

We experience this co-creative relationship hundreds of times each day, but we usually take it for granted without being conscious of the cause and effect relationship inherent within it:

We want to eat; food appears and we eat.

We want to see a movie; we go to the theater and watch the particular movie we want to see.

We want to fly to New York; we board a plane that just happens to take us there.

These are not miracles. It is the way life organizes around desire and manifestation.

As this relationship between what we want and what we receive becomes more apparent, we can become much more intentional in exploring what we want. The process itself of feeling what we truly want becomes the key element in attracting and receiving what we want. For example, the person who knows from an early age that he or she wants to be an actor and passionately follows that desire is usually the one who ends up being chased by the paparazzi.

In the Biblical quote of 'Ask and it shall be given,' the 'asking' is the same as 'identifying and feeling' what we want. The desire itself sets in motion the manifestation of that desire.

Six:
Feeling and following what we want requires that we distinguish between our 'hidden conditioned wants' and our 'conscious heart-felt wants'.

To be guided by what we love involves a 'rewiring' from the old paradigm. For example, the old paradigm says that to follow what we love is selfish. It says that, instead of following our own heart intelligence, we should follow reason, belief, custom, addiction, and advertiser's orders. For many, the old paradigm also has within it the belief that life is difficult and dangerous or that we are sinners and separate from God or that our purpose here is to sacrifice ourselves for some reason that always seems to be lost in fine print.

These old paradigm thoughts are not necessarily easy to replace because they are often hidden within our subconscious minds. They also have several thousand years of tradition behind them and a lifetime of patterning.

To counteract these obstacles requires that we become sensitive to our own internal guidance system. This system is based on first identifying what we are feeling, thinking, and doing right now in the present moment. We must become a nonjudgmental witness to this which means that we don't label what we are feeling, thinking, and doing as 'good' or 'bad.'

This non-judgmental witnessing is critical. If I am feeling angry, thinking that I have been victimized, and pounding my fist on the steering wheel of my car, I must be able to identify this without thinking that I 'shouldn't' be feeling, thinking, or doing this. The fact is that I am.

But, once I am in touch with my own feelings, thoughts, and actions in any given moment, instead of dwelling on them, I am now in a position to ask myself what it is that I WANT to feel, think, and do.

This is a pivotal moment. It is the opening through which we become more deliberate in creating our own life experience. It is the moment in which we can access joy because the question itself, 'What do I WANT to feel, think or do?' automatically switches our attention to what we would enjoy. And what we give our attention to is what we attract to us.

Using the previous example:

I'm feeling really angry.

That guy just swerved in front of me and cut me off.

And here I am pounding my hand on the steering wheel.

Okay, that's what is happening. Given that, what do I

want?

What I want to feel is: grateful that it didn't end up in a crash.

What I want to think is: 'life is a precious and this guy's dangerous driving reminded me of that.'

What I want to do is: pay more attention to my own driving because when that happened, I wasn't really watching the road.

I don't want to shift from being angry to being grateful just because I think that I 'shouldn't' be angry. I want to shift because, in that instance, I feel better when I'm grateful than I do when I'm angry. At the same time, I don't want to shift until I allow myself to feel my anger, or otherwise, I just end up repressing it. Our internal guidance system is based on 'what feels better,' this or that? What feels more joyful, this or that? What feels more in alignment with my own integrity, this or that? And we first have to be in touch with what we are feeling before we can make this distinction.

The act itself of switching my attention to what feels better to me feels better to me. The act of asking what I want feels better to me than not asking this question. And, not only does asking the question feel better, but, actually answering the question and identifying what I want sets in motion the Law of Attraction: I draw to me what I want. If I fully 'feel' my desire to feel grateful, I attract to me gratitude. If I really want to drive more carefully, the desire to do so manifests in my driving more carefully.

In simplistic terms, we are designed to follow in every moment what feels good or right or true and to veer away from what feels bad, false, or dissonant. Knowing and then choosing what feels good, right, or joyful to us is what it means to be 'heart-directed.'

Seven:
What we are manifesting in our lives that we don't want can be used to clarify what we do want.

When we truly want something that we don't have, the Law of Attraction says that we are not yet a vibrational match to that which we want. We resist receiving what we want by sending mixed signals into the 'unified energetic field' (which some people call 'God') and get back mixed results. If we want more money, but believe that we aren't worthy enough to receive it, it is unlikely that more money will appear. If we want an intimate relationship, but fear being intimate because of having been hurt in the past, that 'door' won't open.

Not receiving what we want provides us with greater clarity as to what we do want. We experience 'contrast': the gap between what we want and what we have right now. This contrast is essential. Without it there would be no differentiation between what we want and don't want. For example, war brings with it a desire for peace. Hunger sharpens the longing to be fed. Unhappiness quickens the quest to be happy.

This process is a never ending, upward spiral. As we move upwards on it, we begin receiving what we truly want, more and more quickly. We also become more grateful for what we receive because we are receiving 'consciously.' We become more creative as the gap decreases between the idea and the act. Joy increases as 'joy begets joy.'

Then something interesting happens.

 Eight:
In the 'higher' energetic states of love, joy, integrity, gratitude, etc. the actual experience of who we are changes dramatically. We go from thinking we are separated from everything to experiencing that we are connected to everything.

As I move into higher states of joy and happiness, I automatically begin to redefine who I am, based on the new experiences that I am having. While maintaining my separate identity, I, at the same time, experience that I am connected to everything else. And as this occurs, I am still on that never ending upward spiral of desire and manifestation.

But what 'I' want changes because of the interconnectedness which I feel towards everything else. In a higher energetic state, my 'I' becomes much more inclusive of others than when I am in a lower energetic state. Therefore, what I want turns automatically into what I want for the greater good of all. If I want happiness for myself, it will include my wanting happiness for others: I am those others.

So, following our heart-felt desires does not lead to narcissism and endless personal consumption. It leads to community and greater connection.

Community is created by much more than geographical proximity. It is created by people supporting each other in feeling, and following what each individual truly wants in any given moment. This leads to joyful individuals who experience their connection to each other, as well as to nature and to their own internal experiences. In this paradigm shift, the individual moves from a being in a competitive mindset to a collective cooperative mindset.

As a species, we are hanging in the balance between this paradigm shift from competition to cooperation. Our future on this planet is being determined in this present moment by how each one of us is making this shift.

 *A summary of the above: No child is born a sinner*

We are vibratory beings.
We vibrate at both higher and lower frequencies.
When we are vibrating at higher frequencies,
We feel good,
We know we are good,
And we do things that feel good to ourselves and to
others.
When we vibrate at lower frequencies,
We lose touch with our goodness,
We feel bad,
And we do things that feel bad to ourselves and to others.

No child is born a sinner in need of redemption.
This doesn't change as the child ages.
An adult can't suddenly turn into a bad or good person. We are all
good by nature.

But we can vibrate at lower frequencies and lose touch with our good-
ness. We can act out of the illusion that we are bad,
unloved,
separate,
and unworthy,
and, in doing so, create a living hell.
But this does not make us bad.
It only means that we are bad at remembering who we are
And that we are untrained in raising our vibrational frequency at
will.

This reality that life is joyful by nature is absolute
rather than relative.
No one has the power to change it.
We can act within that reality or create a separate reality
of our own design.
These separate realities are always painful.
The ultimate reality is always joyful.
There are no exceptions to this rule.

Heart Circles are made up of people wanting to support each other in feeling and following what they love.

If you want to be a musician, hang out with other musicians. If you want to play soccer, join a soccer team. To learn anything, be with others who are as passionate as you are about what you want to do.

To individually move out of the old paradigm of separation, struggle, and survival to a new paradigm of unity, cooperation, and flow requires support. It is easy to talk about the concept of following what your heart truly wants, but doing it requires much more than talking, reading books, or going to weekend seminars. The theory is relatively simple but applying it takes constant trial and error learning over time. It also takes commitment, courage, and tremendous perseverance. We are actually changing how our brains are wired as we re-imagine who we are and how life can be if lived from this place of infinite creativity. We are ***consciously*** participating in our own evolutionary development.

45

Heart Circles are ongoing weekly or bimonthly support groups that are designed as experiential learning environments in which we help each other to clarify the direction that we each want to take in our lives. By meeting weekly or bimonthly, this kind of cooperative support is available to us on an ongoing basis: Heart Circles can continue meeting for weeks, months, or years, according to what each member needs and wants. They are self-facilitated and self-organized. It is up to each member to hold the group focus on what he or she wants from the infinite possibilities available in any given moment.

It is easy to speak of love and cooperation when our stomachs are full, our bank accounts positive, and no one's life is on the line. But, as social change continues to accelerate, none of this is guaranteed. Strong community support allows us to be more flexible and responsive to what does occur externally because, with this kind of social support, we are less likely to react out of fear. We become part of the safety net that close friends create together.

Heart Circles also provide space for us to receive objective group feedback as we explore what we want to create in our lives. This feedback is not analytical; other group members don't offer back what they 'think' about what another is sharing. They offer back what they are 'feeling.' If we speak about what we want with passion and enthusiasm, others in the Circle will feel this and be 'moved.' If what we share has no passion, members will feel that too. Group feedback can often allow us better access to the actual depth and clarity of our own longing. If no one is moved by what we are sharing, we may want to quiet our minds, go deeper, and continue inquiring into the mystery of our own calling. And if everyone is moved, the others in the Circle actually amplify our expression of what we want. Manifestation quickens with this amplification.

Also, by exploring what we want in our weekly Heart Circle, we can become more motivated and adept at identifying what we want outside of Circle in our day-to- day lives. We get better at being guided by our own longing, creativity, and gratitude, rather than our conditioned or strategic responses to life.

Exploring what we want in Circle also allows us to look at our doubts and fears relating to what we want. At that point, we have a greater opportunity to understand when we are not in a state of 'vibrational match' to what we want so that we can better align what we want with our beliefs, feelings, and actions.

Heart Circles also offer an environment in which to learn 'non-attachment,' exploring how our happiness is not dependent upon our getting what we want. Members have an opportunity to look at the difference between falsely defining 'non-attachment' as 'giving up our desires,' rather than 'giving up the *need* to have our desires fulfilled.'

Joy is created not by what we are receiving in life; this would make happiness conditional on our getting what we want. An entirely different process creates joy: first we feel fully what we desire, which, itself, makes us feel alive and passionate. Then life organizes itself around our desires, if we are in vibrational alignment with that desire. And, finally, we are able to consciously 'let in' or receive what we desire, which brings with it a sense of gratitude, humility, and wonder. Everything we receive in life becomes a gift from life. Even not receiving what we want becomes a gift because it provides contrast so that we can better align ourselves with what we truly desire. Each part of this process is independently designed to allow us to feel joyful.

Again, all of this is difficult to communicate in words. It is like talking about swimming when you've never been wet. Heart Circles provide an environment to directly experience what these concepts actually mean.

At this evolutionary crossroads in which we are moving from survival-based competition to 'thrival-based' cooperation, our survival may be dependent upon making this shift.

If tomorrow, we hear that a meteor large enough to destroy a continent is going to indisputably strike our earth in thirty days, how would we cope with this impending catastrophe?

One coping strategy would obviously be 'denial': "This can't happen; the scientists are wrong; I am not going to even think about it."

Others would experience panic, paralysis, depression, or hysteria and be dysfunctional for the next thirty days.

And still others would respond by finding ways to profit from the situation: selling emergency products and plans at inflated prices to would-be survivors.

But there would be another strategy that millions of people would employ. They would open their hearts as they have never opened them before: enjoying each moment as it's given, staying present and alert, processing their own fears while giving solace to others, and following the intelligence that always comes when the heart is open.

Today we are faced with a situation much like this meteor strike, but with three significant differences. First, instead of one meteor crashing toward us, there are many. Second, instead of having thirty days before these meteors strike, we have none; they have already struck. Third, these meteors are more like time release capsules striking our earth in that their explosive impact ripples out over time, rather than happening in one devastating bang.

Right now, civilization as we know it is undergoing irreversible and dramatic change due to unprecedented processes set in motion long ago. We are all aware of what these processes are, and have been warned repeatedly about their consequences by the experts who study them.

And we will all continue to respond to these processes in our varying ways: with ongoing denial, emotional dysfunction, and senseless profiteering or with a radical shift into cooperation, compassion, and love.

The decreasing supply of oil and the ever-increasing demand for it is just beginning to strike our world's economies. And, currently, the race for control of what oil remains is focused on fierce national competition, rather than cooperative world conservation and creative action.

Global warming is not something that may happen later: the Arctic ice is melting now. Weather patterns are changing dramatically, causing climatologists to sound more like science fiction writers than weather forecasters.

While our attention has been focused elsewhere, other meteor-like explosions have already occurred. These have resulted in the annihilation of a significant portion of the Amazon rain forest and of many of the world's animal and plant species. We have depleted huge amounts of our planetary freshwater reserves and our farmable topsoil. Nothing suggests a reversal of these ecological trends.

Nuclear weapons, biological weapons, machetes, bullets, and bombs: we have slain hundreds of millions of our own species in the last 90 years. There is nothing to suggest that this slaughter will end anytime soon.

The foremost public health concern today is the bird flu virus. Health officials are in agreement that it is not a question of 'if' a pandemic will break out, but when.

Everyone who has ever played Monopoly knows that the game is always over before it actually ends: one player buys enough red hotels to cause the other players to be renters. The game goes on, but the rich player grows richer while the other players are wiped out. In today's global Monopoly Game, a tiny fraction of the world's population holds a majority of its wealth. This game is falsely called 'free market capitalism' because the few with the red hotels have a monopoly on the media and can call it anything they want. But this is not free market capitalism. It is Mega-Corporate Monopoly and the game is already over for the poorest people in the world.

Any one of these challenges is capable of collapsing global systems that are in place for us now. Together, they could combine into what some call 'singularity,' a situation in which all of these divergent nightmares happen within the same general time period, each affecting the emergence of the other.

As bleak as this may be, it is our response to what is happening now that is more important than how the times will unfold in the future. This is because it is our response that will help determine how the times actually unfold. Are we responding with denial, dysfunction, and destructive profiteering? Or are we using the dangerous times to open our hearts to creative change on a scale that the world has never seen before?

Dangerous times dramatically reflect back to us individually and collectively in terms of what daily choices we are making in life: are we in denial or seeing clearly? Are we frozen in shock or alive in love? Are we living just for ourselves or expanding the definition of 'self' to include everything else? Are we living the Great Giveaway or the Great Getaway?

So, yes, the times are dangerous. There are dragons every-where: scary ones. But these dragons give a face to fear so that we can look it in the eyes. Dragons clarify which emotional state we choose to live in during any given moment. They provide contrast, and contrast provides choice.

But brave talk about dragons will not take us through the times; nor will theories, nor will any strategy of 'going it alone.' These changes are much too big for that. Fifty-foot waves have little regard for tiny canoes.

To take us through the times, we need 'community.' Community intrinsically means that the people within it feel that it is their community. They belong to it and are known in it. They decide what it becomes. In a worst case scenario, if there is a centralized collapse, we will need to re-create self-sustaining local communities for our survival. In the best-case scenario, we will need self-sustaining local communities because they increase our sense of being loved, needed, and known.

Heart Circles can be used as a basis from which we 'relocalize' our society.

If ten or twenty Heart Circles form and flourish within one town or local area, they can become the foundation on which self-sustaining communities thrive. Two Ashland, Oregon visionaries; Kirsten Liegeman and Dominic Allamano and I have developed a model for how this can be deliberately organized. It is called 'In My Village.'

52

In the 'In My Village' model, all the people in the various Heart Circles have an opportunity to gather together monthly to share a potluck meal and meet each other. At this gathering, time is created for people to talk about creative projects that they are interested in initiating: reading groups, organic gardening clubs, cooperative business ideas, tool sharing banks, joint child care opportunities, anything that people want to do together for mutual benefit.

From these monthly gatherings, projects can emerge spontaneously, involving those people who have passion for them. These projects can evolve with great ease and enjoyment because the people engaged in them already know how to maximize communication and connection with each other because of their involvement in Heart Circles. They also know how to self-organize and self-facilitate these small 'creation circles.' And they all take responsibility for their own emotional states and actions rather than blaming others or playing victim to circumstance.

If this community faces an emergency or if the times bring systemic collapse, there is in place a group of 50 to 100 people who know and respect each other and have a history of working together cooperatively. Their shared experience of unity replaces ideology. They self organize their own 'community within a community' so that they can fulfill what is most wanted and needed in the local area where it is birthed. The primary function of the "In My Village" model and the Heart Circles within it is always to support the creative aspirations of the people who form these groups.

Fighting with each other and plundering natural resources are no longer viable options for the inhabitants of Planet Earth. That dinosaur is dead. The "In My Village" model is one alternative that resonates with this 21st Century reality.

In summary, there are five specific benefits of being in a Heart Circle.

Manifesting: In a Heart Circle, you have others who support you in manifesting joy in your life.

In Heart Circles, we can look at what we are attracting to us so that we can see where we are giving our attention. Then we can determine if we want what we are attracting and if we don't, we can focus on what we really want until it shows up to replace that which we have been attracting. This applies to everything in life, how we want to feel, what we want to think, what we want to have, and what we want to do. It becomes both a psychological and a spiritual practice.

 **_Friends_: _In a Heart Circle, you have other friends who will celebrate with you the Journey of Life._**

As children, most of us had the experience of saying to a playmate, "Do you want to be my friend?" The question was pretty straightforward. So was the answer; it was either a simple 'ok' or 'no.' As four year olds, we knew exactly what we were asking for. It was always specific to that playmate whom we were asking. If there was agreement, it was because both could feel a certain resonance that would allow a friendship to develop. These friendships were intentional and extremely important in our early childhood development.

A Heart Circle is a place for adults to create friendship intentionally. It begins with a straightforward question similar to the one you asked as a child. You approach a handful of people with whom you already feel a certain resonance, and say, "Do you want to build a deeper friendship together?" Heart Circles offer a structure that supports friendship because the people involved have all of the necessary ingredients required to support the growth of friendships: spending real time together, being open and honest, working through conflicts, caring about each other, and simply being committed to the friendships.

Building friendships deliberately is, for many people, an innovative concept. Did you ever attend a class in school on how to be a friend? Did you ever learn how to be open and honest, how to resolve conflict, how to be more empathetic and caring? As you moved into the job market, did you ever find a job where the climate of friendship was recognized as being as important to the business bottom line as profit itself? Have you noticed that most mass entertainment doesn't support personal connections and most housing structures encourage separation?

Because of the frenetic pace of modern life, many people simply don't have time to develop deep friendships. Yet friendships are one of the most valuable forms of 'social capital' that we have as a society. They are portals to a greater connection beyond the 'self.' They are enjoyable and essential to physical, mental, emotional, and spiritual health. Heart Circles support the process of forming and deepening friendships between people who want those kinds of relationships.

 __In Crisis__: In a Heart Circle, you have others who will be there for you if a crisis comes.

A gut wrenching loss, a particularly hard time, a quarrel too dark to digest, a turning point or sudden shock: If any of these come in the middle of the night or at the height of a busy day, do you have friends who will drop everything for you if you call?

If your friends had lost their homes due to a natural disaster, could they come live with you? If jobs disappear because the economy bottoms out, with whom will you share what you have? If the bird flu becomes a pandemic, whom will you continue to touch?

It is often said about emergencies that getting through them depends on having a plan before they appear. The interesting thing is that it is not just the plan that helps people to survive, it is the planning process itself that is valuable. Creating a plan implies that the planners accept the possibility that a disaster could occur. Therefore, if it does happen, the shock from the surprise is minimized and it is often the shock that keeps us from responding appropriately.

Whether the crisis is personal or collective, whether it is short term or long term, having friends who will show up for you is vital. Heart Circles are designed to include discussions about these kinds of contingencies.

 In Community: In a Heart Circle you have others with whom to build sustainable communities.

Being in a community allows us to be known to each other, to work and play together, to be part of a greater whole. In a community, we have friends we can trust with our lives. We have support for following what we love and what we want to create.

A healthy community comes with the responsibility to continuously turn it into what we want it to be. In what new ways do we want to learn, do business, grow food, raise children, be artistic, retire, rehabilitate, defend, and play and grieve together?

We also have the challenge of re-localizing our communities so that more of what we consume and need in areas such as food, power, and capital are locally controlled, rather than being thousands of miles out of our control.

Heart Circles provide a nucleus for this kind of cooperative creativity.

 In The Future: *In a Heart Circle, you have others who'll be responding with you to the changes that are coming.*

Being in a Heart Circle doesn't require having any one particular set of views of times in which we live with one set of particular responses to events and problems. It does encourage people to discover what their own views are and then live from day to day in accordance with those views. In this way, we create a 'context' from which we make many of our daily decisions.

For example, if we think that global warming is, in part, being caused by fossil fuel emissions, this belief will affect the kind of cars which we drive.

One particularly poignant image that can be used to further clarify the meaning of having a 'contextual understanding of the times' is that of those U.S. embassy staff members in Saigon at the end of the Vietnam War playing tennis while the Viet Cong were entering the city. Tennis is a wonderful game, but knowing what's going on in the neighborhood is essential in our deciding when to play.

How to Create
A Dynamic
Heart Circle

How to Create
A Dynamic
Heart Circle

A Heart Circle begins with your interest in being in a Circle. This book can be used to develop a clear understanding of the theory and structure of Heart Circles so that you may decide if being in one is something you want. If it is you can take the following steps:

For individuals

First, identify one or two people in your life who meet the following criteria:

- You like and respect each other. You don't have to be good friends, but you must share a certain resonance together.

- You have a sense that they would be interested in being in a Heart Circle with you.

- You live in the same general area.

Second, get together informally to talk about forming a Heart Circle, as laid out in this book.

- What do you like about the possibilities of being in a Heart Circle together?

- What are your doubts?

- Who else do you want to invite to a preliminary Heart Circle meeting? (Up to eight people.)

- Where might you meet and how often?

- What is the mix of people you want in your Circle: all men or all women? Mixed gender? Couples?

- When do you want to have a Preliminary Heart Circle meeting to set up an experimental eight week Heart Circle?

Invite all of these people to this meeting, after creating a time and location for it.

Third, have a preliminary Heart Circle meeting or a series of meetings with up to eight people whom you have decided to invite: (It may take more than one meeting to formulate how you want to proceed) make sure that they are familiar with the basic information in this book before they come to the meeting.

- Determine who wants to proceed with an initial eight week Heart Circle experiment after talking about what a Heart Circle is.

- Decide when and where you want to meet and how often: weekly or every other week? (Meeting monthly does not work: if one person misses a meeting, it is two months between Circles.)

- Go over the Heart Circle Agreements and decide on with which ones you agree. If you have other agreements that you wish to make that are not listed in this book, discuss those, as well.

- Agree that you will all help to facilitate your group together, using this manual as a guide.

Fourth, convene and enjoy your first Heart Circle meeting, using the agenda and guidelines found on pages 72 to 86.

Fifth, at the end of the eight weeks, decide who wants to continue at the next agreed upon period of time!

For existing organizations or networks

First, insure that several key people in the organization are introduced to the Heart Circle idea by reading this book.

Second, have a preliminary meeting with these key people to discuss whether your organization wants to explore setting up an experimental Heart Circle.

Third, if so, identify four to eight people who are interested and who resonate with each other. Follow the same five steps as listed above.

Fourth, if the initial Heart Circle is successful, introduce the concept to others in the organization so that they can form their own Circles.

Here are eleven critical agreements involved with being in Heart Circle together.

All relationships have spoken and unspoken agreements that help those relationships flourish. For example, in most business relationships, there is the unspoken agreement for both parties to be honest with each other. In marriage, there is the verbalized agreement during the marriage ceremony that the couple will be monogamous.

In Heart Circles, there are also certain basic agreements that allow the Circle to function effectively. As important as these agreements are, they cannot be imposed on anyone: they are what their name implies, agreements. As such, they need to be discussed and then agreement needs to be reached through consensus. This is best done at the Preliminary Heart Circle Meeting so that each member has a clear understanding of what being in the Circle actually entails.

 ## *Confidentiality*

Because a Heart Circle is a place in which members are free to speak intimately about what is happening in their personal lives, it is essential to have agreements involving 'confidentiality.' The general rule is 'what happens in Circle stays in Circle.' This does not necessarily apply to information shared in the group that is already common knowledge. If there is any gray area around what is confidential and what is not, always check back with the group members for clarification before sharing with someone outside the group.

Within each Circle, members must grapple with their own definition of confidentiality and then create their own agreements around maintaining it. Once these agreements are in place, they must be honored. Breaking confidentiality will break the group. Always.

 ## *No Third Party Talk*

During Heart Circle, talking analytically or negatively about other people who aren't present in Circle will significantly lower the overall vitality and integrity of the group.

Also, if you have an issue with anyone in your Circle, your commitment is to always speak to that person directly about that issue, rather than with others inside or outside of your Circle. This agreement replaces 'third party' talk with direct, honest communication.

Taking Responsibility

When speaking within the Circle, taking responsibility for your own experience will keep the Circle strong. Speak only for yourself, instead of for others. Use 'I' statements, rather than 'we' or 'you' statements. Reflect on how you have created any situation you are in rather than being a victim of that situation. Find out what you want in relationship to your situation, rather than putting all of your attention on the drama inherent in it.

Resolve Conflicts Directly and Quickly

Resolve conflicts that may arise within your Circle as soon as they arise, rather than letting them crystallize. Be open, direct, and clear about what you want and what you are feeling, while listening compassionately to what others want and feel.

No Drugs or Alcohol in Circle

As with driving, don't mix drugs, alcohol, or smoking while you are meeting in your Heart Circle. What you do outside of Circle is up to you, but, in Circle, exploring how you can consciously transform your emotional and energetic state is impossible if you have already used drugs or alcohol to do so.

Notification

If you can't be at a particular Heart Circle meeting or if you are going to be late, ensure that someone in the group is notified before the meeting starts. Waiting for someone to show up greatly affects the quality of the meeting. It also means that the person who doesn't notify the group is minimizing his or her own importance in the Circle.

If someone arrives late, consider using this as an opportunity to explore what each member 'feels' about this, rather than what each member 'thinks' about this. For example, one person may say that he or she feels anxious when another doesn't show up, rather than saying that that he or she 'thinks' it is irresponsible for that person to arrive late. If someone misses the meeting without notification, you can use a few minutes of the next meeting to ask the person who was absent what he or she experienced about not notifying anyone. What was he or she thinking and feeling? Non-judgmental communication only, please.

Commitment

Heart Circles will not function well if they are 'drop in' groups in which no one knows who will show up in Circle and who will not. Decide together on a certain number of weeks that you want to 'experiment' with being in Circle together. Eight-week commitments work well; it often takes that long for a group to really 'gel' and establish itself as a functioning group. During this time, making Heart Circle meetings a high priority is essential to making Circle effective.

At the end of the eight weeks, members can then decide individually if they want to continue and for how long.

Closure

If someone decides to leave the Heart Circle, it is essential to have a prior agreement in place around adequate 'closure' for the person leaving. Closure consists of giving everyone in Circle a chance to express his or her feelings and thoughts around that person's involvement in the group and the fact that he or she is leaving it. The person leaving should have this same opportunity.

Closure is never about judging a person's reasons for leaving. It is simply a process of consciously and kindly ending a specific relationship before something new begins.

Some of the questions to explore during closure are:

1. What worked and didn't work for you while in Circle?

2. What are you feeling about leaving?

3. Is there anything you need to say to anyone in the group or to the group as a whole to feel 'complete' in your leaving?

4. What is each individual feeling about that person leaving? (Be aware of the difference between 'thoughts or judgments' and 'feelings.')

Consensus

There will be numerous times in the life of a Heart Circle in which group decisions will have to be made: letting new people into the group, changing meeting times, etc. These kinds of decisions are best made through consensus in which everyone must agree. This is because once a person is a member of a Heart Circle, it is 'his' or 'her' Circle. Everyone has full say in what happens in Circle or else that ownership is meaningless. If there isn't consensus in terms of an issue, keep working on it until there is.

Confrontation and Accountability

Heart Circles are not about confronting each other or holding each other accountable. Those kinds of groups exist elsewhere. In Heart Circles, members can ask for support in reference to doing something, but, in general, members are accountable to themselves. Members may ask for feedback in relation to an issue, but, without that invitation, giving uninvited feedback is trespassing in another's personal space. Mind your own joy!

Staying Within Time Boundaries

If you say that you are going to end Heart Circle at a certain time, end it at that time. The same goes with starting at a certain time. If there is a change, get everybody's agreement before changing that time. This is more important than it may seem. A certain trust and safety is established when everyone knows and then honors when a meeting begins and ends. If people want to extend the meeting at closure time, take a moment or two to develop consensus on a specific additional time period: "Is everyone OK with going another 15 minutes?" Then honor that new closing time.

In addition to these critical agreements, there are also some suggestions which you may want to consider together.

Meeting Environment

The quality of the environment that develops in Heart Circle will affect the quality of your experience. The best place to meet is in cozy homes where there are no outside interruptions and where there is comfortable seating (on the floor or in chairs and sofas).

Meeting in restaurants or in public places usually does not provide enough privacy and focus for what a Heart Circle needs.

Food

It is best to not eat food while in Circle; it distracts from the group focus. If this is not clear, test it out for your-selves as an experiment. Try eating while you meet and see what happens to the quality of your experience. Also, it is best to not meet after eating large meals. Sharing fruit or snacks after Circle closes works well.

Privacy

Ensure that no one can overhear what is happening within your Circle while meeting and that people don't walk into your meeting space once your Circle begins. This is especially important because you may be meeting in each other's homes where other household members live who are not in Circle.

No Tables

Sit in comfortable chairs, sofas, or on cushions on the floor with empty spaces between you. Sitting around a table encourages taking action together. Sitting around empty space encourages being together.

Here is the suggested agenda to follow for a two-hour Heart Circle meeting.

Heart Circles are amazing, not so much because of what you 'do' while you are in them, but because of what you 'observe and consciously experience' while in them. And what you observe and experience is 'you': your thought patterns, emotional responses, subtle fluctuations in your energetic field, your desires, beliefs, and intentions. In a Heart Circle, you receive a reflection back to you of what is happening in your life so that you can adjust your life according to what you see. In short, you have an opportunity to become more conscious of how you are raising or lowering your own energy levels throughout your day.

You also have an opportunity in Heart Circles to 'feel' what is happening within the group energetically: not to be confused with making judgments about what is happening.

Are people speaking intimately and authentically?
Does the group itself feel good or is there tension?
Is everyone involved and enthusiastic?
Is there high energy or low energy as the group progresses?

By being sensitive to how the group feels energetically, you can better raise the energy when it is low and sustain the energy when it is high.

Therefore, the Heart Circle 'agenda' is meant to be a flowing guideline, rather than a formalized procedure set in stone. You don't need a stopwatch or a conversation cop to regulate what happens in Circle, but you do need a focused sensitivity to stay within parameters outlined here. As your Heart Circle follows this format over time, you can make adjustments based upon your own experience of what works and doesn't work as you find your own group rhythms and preferences.

As with life, the key to every Heart Circle meeting is your intention to enjoy being in it.

HEART CIRCLE AGENDA: 2 hours

TUNE-IN: 2-4 minutes

CHECK IN: 2 or 3 minutes for each member

OPEN DISCUSSION: 20 minutes discussion of one of the 26 questions (page 87).

EXPLORING WHAT EACH MEMBER WANTS: 10 to 15 minutes for each member

OPEN DISCUSSION: 10 minutes discussion of the same question you began with

CLOSURE: 2-4 minutes

Begin by sitting in silence together and 'tuning-in': (2-4 minutes)

Heart Circle begins with everyone sitting in a circle together in silence, hands held, eyes closed for 2 or 3 minutes. Clear your mind, get into present time, consciously feel what you are feeling.

People have consistently shared that this tune-in process has a common progression: in the first minute or so of silence, your focus is often consumed by the spin of your own mental chatter. Then, there is a shift from 'thinking' to 'feeling' your own body or emotions. You become more 'present.' Then there is a jump into feeling the presence of others in the Circle with you as you feel the collective energetic field.

There are no 'shoulds' in this process. If someone doesn't get past the chatter of their minds, it means that what they are thinking is important and can be shared with the group in the 'check-in.' The same is true for individual emotions. The key is to be aware of where you are, rather than where you think you should be in this process.

A short check-in allows everyone to say what he or she is feeling and wanting as the Circle begins. (2-3 minutes each)

Each person takes 2 or 3 minutes to 'check-in.' You can either go around the circle 'in order' or have the order be 'random' as each person checks-in when ready to speak.

A check-in covers any one or all of the following:

1. What are you feeling right now?

2. What has happened since the last meeting that is significant to you?

3. What do you want during this meeting?

The check-in is best kept short. If it goes longer than a few minutes each, it blurs the line between 'checking-in' and the rest of the Heart Circle process. Having short check-ins also allows members the opportunity to be concise and direct in communicating what they are feeling or wanting without having to go into their 'story' involving these feelings or experiences. This is a wonderful skill to have in communicating with others inside or outside of Circle.

Check-ins 'ground' each person in the present moment. Members notify everyone else what they are bringing into the Circle, as the meeting begins.

For example, someone may come into the circle and say, 'I am feeling anxious. My father ended up in the hospital yesterday and needs some surgery.' This information allows everyone to know immediately what this member is experiencing. The meeting will organically arrange itself to accommodate him or her as the meeting progresses. If this isn't shared at the start of the meeting, everyone may sense that something is going on with this person, but not know what it actually is.

This takes us back to the old paradigm practiced in many school classrooms. A classmate could come to class emotionally devastated by some family event and never be asked by the teacher or other students what happened. Because we never used 'check-ins' in these kind of social settings, we subconsciously learned how to separate our personal lives from our social lives. We began playing roles, rather than being 'real' because there was no encouragement to share what we were 'really' thinking and feeling.

What most people find after doing Heart Circle check-ins is how strange it is to start any kind of meeting without them. They find themselves thinking, as a business meeting starts, 'Wait a minute! Aren't we going to check-in with each other first?' On some level, we are all sensitive to what others are feeling. When this is intentionally articulated, we don't have to guess what others are experiencing because there is emotional transparency in our communication.

With this said, check-ins are always optional in Heart Circles. You can 'pass' if you don't want to share what you're feeling. It is your Circle.

Choose one of the 26 Questions and discuss your answers to it (20 minutes) (see page 87)

Some questions elicit intellectual answers: what are your thoughts or beliefs about a certain subject. For example, what is the best way to get across town during rush hour? What do you think we should do about global warming? These questions invite rational responses and involve opinions, judgments, facts, and beliefs.

Other questions elicit more heuristic answers: what are you feeling about a certain subject. For example, what do you 'want' for dinner tonight? How was your vacation? These questions invite emotive responses and usually involve feelings, desires, intuition, and emotions.

Most human activity originates in our emotive neural centers because the actions which we take are always preceded by motivation and intention. We do what we do based on what we 'feel,' rather than what we 'think.' For example, even if we do something because we 'think' it is the 'right' thing to do, that thought must 'feel' right to us. We always 'want' something before taking an action that we 'think' will fulfill that want, even if that 'want' is subconscious.

Our public educational system is centered on 'thinking.' It not only offers little help in educating students about what motivates their moment to moment actions, but, by this omission, it also teaches them to avoid looking at what motivates them. If we don't know what motivates us and if we don't know what we truly want when we take certain actions, we have no 'compass' to guide us. We end up being controlled by our own subconscious wants and conditioned thinking because we haven't been encouraged or trained to investigate what our motivations are for doing what we do.

A Heart Circle is a sophisticated educational structure that supports people who want to intentionally explore what they are feeling and wanting before they take action. Are they being motivated by fear or love? What are the wants underneath the wants? For example, I may want to go to a social gathering because I want to enjoy being with the people who will be there or I may go only because I feel obligated to go. Knowing what motivates me gives me greater freedom of choice. Is this sense of obligation real or something I am making up?

The 26 Heart Circle Questions are designed to help you clarify what you are wanting, feeling, and intuiting. The process for using them in your Heart Circle is simple: together, choose one of these questions to discuss after the check-in. Read the accompanying text that follows the question which you have chosen. Discuss for twenty minutes what everyone is feeling in relation to the question.

These 26 questions are also designed to bring your attention to many subtle aspects involved in small group dynamics. Through this process, you will learn much about how to make your Heart Circle more effective and enjoyable. Many of the questions include a simple 'experiment' which you can conduct during that particular Heart Circle meeting. (At the end of the meeting, there is another ten minute time period in which to find out how everyone 'experienced the experiment.'

A major portion of Heart Circle is spending time exploring what each member wants in life. (10 to 15 minutes each)

The act of identifying and feeling what we want or what we love serves two functions:

It instantly and automatically raises our energy level. Feeling what we want feels good; it's internally inspiring; it's the spark of life itself.

It sets in motion the Law of Attraction in that what we focus on is what we draw to us. Focus on what we want, and what we want is attracted to us.

When we understand these two basic functions, we can participate in them more intentionally. If we want to feel more inspired and alive, we can simply direct more of our attention to what it is that we truly want. If we want to receive in life more of what we want, rather than more of what we don't want, we simply become clearer or more conscious of what our wants are.

If this sounds simple, it is. We complicate it by not grasping the simplicity inherent within it. Each day we make decisions on thousands of things that we want, and most of those things occur simply because we want them and because this is how life is organized. We want to eat. We do. We want to go to the bathroom, we do. We want to stand up, we do. But we may do all of this unconsciously, rather than consciously.

Heart Circles are essentially about making these two functions conscious so that we can feel more alive more of the time and so that we can manifest what we want in life, rather than what we don't want.

In the Heart Circle agenda, each member takes 10 to 15 minutes each to feel and talk about what he or she wants in his or her life. There are two different ways to do this.

First, we can divide life arbitrarily into different areas and ask what each person wants in relation to that area:

What do you want in relationship to:

- *Your partnership or marriage:* If you don't have a partner, do you want one? If you have a partner, do you want more intimacy, more fun, more sex, better communication? What do you want? It can be anything.

- *Your family:* If you have children, do you want to spend more time with them? Less time? If you have a brother, do you want to call him this week? What do you want in relation to your cousin Harry?

- *Your individual friends:* What do you want in relation to those with whom you are closest?

- *Your community:* You can define this term however you want and it can include political or civic involvement. It can also include your neighborhood or the people with whom you work.

- *Your work:* Do you love to go to work? If not, what do you want? If you do love your work, what do you want?

- *Your money:* How do you want to manage you income? Or your lack of income? How do you want to spend or save your money?

- *Your play/leisure:* This includes vacations, sports, connection to nature, hobbies, and anything else that you love to do for play and rejuvenation.

- *Your health:* This includes your physical, emotional, mental, energetic, and spiritual health. They are all listed under 'health' because each area affects and overlaps the other; i.e. our mental health affects our physical health and our spiritual health affects our emotional health.

- *Your learning/creativity:* What do you want to learn next and how do you want to express yourself creatively?

- *The details of your life:* This includes taking care of your home, car, clothes, etc.

Each Heart Circle meeting can focus on what members want in any one of these areas. Pick another area during your next meeting.

The second way to facilitate this part of the Heart Circle agenda is to keep the 'What do you want?' question open-ended. Let each individual talk about what he or she wants without structuring the question. In this way, members would start out talking about their week or their jobs or what they are feeling about subjects that are important to them, and from there, speak about what they want. For example, one member may start talking about tension that he or she is feeling in reference to a family member. This will lead that person to 'feel into' what he or she wants in order to resolve the tension.

Both structured and non-structured ways of looking at what you want are effective. Experiment with both.

To better facilitate this process, consider these things:

It's up to everyone in the Circle to keep the general focus on what each member wants. If someone spends all of his or her time sharing his or her 'story,' rather than what he or she wants, anyone can say to that person at any time something like, 'Given this, what do you want?'

At the same time, it's important that people have the opportunity to share whatever their 'stories' are. This can include both the circumstances of what is happening in their lives and what they are feeling about those circumstances. If not given this space, the person sharing will feel that he or she is not being heard and what that individual truly wants will not 'emerge.' There is a delicate balance here.

'Thinking' about what we want and actually 'feeling' what we want are very different. The power in manifesting what we want comes from feeling our desires, rather than thinking about them. When others in the Circle can feel what another member wants, it is a good indicator that that member is speaking from that feeling place in his or her heart.

The more specific a 'want' is the more likely it is that we will feel it. If we say that an individual wants to be happy or more relaxed, he or she can be encouraged to look for what specific things he or she wants that makes that person happy or that relaxes him or her. Go for the one hundred small things instead of the one big thing.

If someone says that he or she does not know what he or she wants, encourage the member to stay with that question until he or she feels 'something' that he or she wants in that particular area. The 'I don't know' is never a dead end, but, rather, a doorway to find what he or she does know.

It is difficult to know what we want unless we are clear about what we are feeling in that particular moment during which the question is being asked.

Be aware that most of us are conditioned to stay away

from feeling what we truly want. It is not an easy question to answer. Knowing this will help you to have the patience and focus to answer it. On the bright side, the more you ask the question, the easier it becomes to answer it. It is a matter of 'practice.'

Return to the opening question. (10 minutes)

In this 10-minute segment of Circle, go back to the question you began with in your Circle. If, for example, the question was the one about intuition, use this time to talk about your experience of intuition during the meeting. Did opening the Circle with that question affect what you experienced during the Circle?

Closing the Heart Circle after each meeting. (4 minutes)

There is an art in knowing how to close one thing before opening another. This applies to relationships, events, meetings, jobs, locations, sales, computer windows, dying, and most everything else that has a beginning and an end. Closure is taking the time and space to say whatever it is you need to say so that you feel 'complete' in what you are closing. In Heart Circle, closure is not for opening up a new topic; it is for closing the topics that you have opened. It is brief. It requires no more than a few words.

There is a bit of magic involved in this topic of closure and more to it than meets the eye. A meeting has an energetic life of its own, as do all relationships and social gatherings. When it's time for that form to end and something new to begin, consciously ending it, rather than just letting it end, allows for a smooth energetic transition from one form to the next.

Experiment with this process to close your Circle:

As with tuning in, sit together in silence with your hands held and eyes open or closed for a minute or two.

Have members take a few seconds to say one thing they experienced in Circle for which they are grateful AND/OR simply say whether they feel 'complete' or 'incomplete' about being in the Circle that is closing AND/OR say one or two words describing how they are feeling as you close.

"I am grateful for the insight I got during Circle tonight. I am complete. I feel really peaceful!"

"I'm feeling frustrated that I didn't take as much time as I wanted to tonight. I am 'incomplete.' (Acknowledging that you are 'incomplete' somehow makes you 'complete.' Experiment with this to find out if it is true for you.)

Twenty-Six Heart Circle Questions

Twenty-Six
Heart Circle
Questions

Choose one of these experiential questions to discuss for 20 minutes each time you meet in your Heart Circle.

1. In Heart Circle, what if we all agree to speak when we want to rather than in some kind of linear order. Would we have chaos or would it lead to greater joy?

As children, most of us were trained in school to speak in order, to not interrupt when someone else is speaking, and to even raise our hands before speaking. Proponents of this kind of linear order often use moral judgments to justify it, and fear to enforce it: it is 'rude' to interrupt and if you do so, you will be sent to the principal's office. The rationale is that there would be chaos if everyone spoke whenever he or she wanted to.

Yet, if we look at the way friends communicate, there is no linear order. They don't raise their hands and say, 'Excuse me, Linda Jo, but could I speak now?' They replace linear order with an internally guided process that automatically calibrates when it is time to speak and when to listen. It requires a kind of social intelligence that gives everyone freedom to speak whenever he or she wants, while balancing everyone's freedom to do likewise. If someone is speaking and someone else jumps in spontaneously, it is part of the joy of being with friends. If Linda Jo doesn't want to be interrupted by Billy Bob, she can tell him so, and she and Billy Bob will work it out spontaneously. If they can't, someone else will jump in and tell Billy Bob to 'cool it' and let Linda Jo finish or tell Linda Jo that he or she wants to hear what Billy Bob has to say before she continues.

So how do you want to communicate with each other in your Heart Circle?

Experiment: during this Circle, explore this kind of spontaneity where external 'rules' and being 'polite' are replaced with an internal 'tuning-in' to each other. Speak whenever you want to speak, while truly listening to everything that others have to say.

2. Have you been conditioned to withhold your positive responses from people assuming that others don't want to hear them? Do you want to reverse this?

There is a tradition in many African American churches for members of the congregation to spontaneously encourage the preacher to keep preaching. It is a back and forth exchange that fuels the vibrancy of the church service. There is permission and encouragement to share positive responses as they happen.

In daily life, you probably know people who are very loose when it comes to giving spontaneous praise and positive feedback. These people are not to be confused with someone who is using a strategic technique from 'How To Win Friends And Influence People.' Instead, these encouraging ones simply allow praise and positive feedback to spill out of them as they feel it. They don't censure their heart's responses.

We are all 'praisers,' but some people are willing to give their responses freely while others hold back their own responses. Heart Circle is a place in which to practice positive response spontaneity.

For example, someone in Circle can be truly excited about what he or she is sharing. The rest of the group may be excited too, but everyone remains silent. The fear-thoughts often associated with this are "No one is really interested in my spontaneous feedback and maybe they will think I am being 'rude' by interjecting it."

Experiment: during this Circle, periodically probe these kinds of 'feedback silences' by having everyone share his or her held back positive responses after one of these 'silences' occurs.

"The spell was broken and the people let out a 'joyful noise'!"

3. What is your experience when you are being intuitive? What does it feel like to you? Do you want to increase your intuition during this meeting?

Everyone is intuitive; some people have learned to identify and trust their intuition more than other people have. Heart Circle is a place in which to increase your awareness of your innate intuitive capacities.

Intuition comes in flashes then disappears. Intuitive insights are brilliant bursts of information that come 'out of the blue.' Most of us live in a noisy, time driven culture in which words wear heavy boots and people talk with megaphones. In your Heart Circle, do you want to intentionally create an increasingly subtle environment in which the whisper of intuition can better be heard?

Experiment: see if being in touch with simply wanting to be more intuitive has any effect on your being so during this meeting.

4. Have you ever explored your limit in terms of how much happiness or intimacy you can take before you shut it off? When you are happy are you waiting for 'the other shoe to drop'?

Lenn Snyder is a therapist in Ashland, Oregon who has worked extensively with identifying how most of us defend against becoming 'too happy.' Within what many of his friends and clients affectionately call *"Lenn's Law"* is the fact that we develop defenses in early childhood to protect us from feeling the terror that comes from the absence of primary parental bonding. These defenses end up in our closing down or dulling all of our feelings, those associated with pleasure, as well as with pain. Therefore, in adulthood, when we are feeling higher levels of joy and pleasure, these defenses will pop up because feelings themselves are dangerous. To protect us from this danger, we will often do something to take us out of joy, usually without any awareness that we are doing so. In the same way, we will protect ourselves from too much success or intimacy or from 'shining too brightly.'

Just having people around who understand *"Lenn's Law"* is extremely helpful as you work through the double bind associated with it. As everyone shares his or her experience of this, it will become obvious how common it is for people to become frightened when 'things are too good to be true.' To disengage from this pattern is not easy. It requires, first, that we keep exploring how we can deliberately create joy. As joy triggers our subconscious defenses against it, we need to develop our internal ability to 'witness' this internal defensive process. Then we need 'self-soothing' skills that allow us to feel safe in the face of the fear that we are feeling. Heart Circles offer a safe environment in which to explore this.

Experiment: for your 20-minute discussion, give time for all of the members to talk about any personal experiences they have had with Lenn's Law. See if any insights come to you as you listen to others share stories on this subject.

5. What does it mean to be sensitive to the 'energetic dynamics' of the group you are in? Are you aware of your capacity to 'read the energetic level' of the group at any particular moment? Do you want to increase your sensitivity to these levels by talking with each other about them?

As humans, we are vibratory beings. We 'vibrate,' as does everything else in Nature. Knowing this, intellectually, is quite different from feeling it experientially. We can be so consumed by our own thoughts, emotions, and 'busyness' that we don't consciously feel that we are vibrating or feeling our own vibratory connection to everything around us.

It's like the cartoon with the two fish facing each other, as one is saying to the other, "What's all this talk about 'water'?"

Just sitting together in Heart Circle automatically creates an energetic field within the circle that can be felt and studied. As people interact within that field, the field changes:

If everyone is engaged and interested in what is happening in the Circle, the group energy field will grow stronger.

If people are just sharing their thoughts in reference to some topic, rather than sharing what they feel and want, the energy will fall.

If all of the members but one is engaged, the energy will

sag around that person.

If someone says that he or she is coming to group and doesn't show up, there will be an energetic hole in the Circle.

If there is unexpressed tension or conflict between two members in the Circle, it will be energetically palpable.

If it becomes known that someone broke Circle confidentiality, the energy will feel like shattered safety glass.

When someone is speaking about what he or she truly wants, that individual's enthusiasm will feel energetically full. When someone is speaking about what he or she has been conditioned to want, that member's words will feel energetically flat.

These are just a few examples of the energetic fluctuations which occur in any group. Some people will 'feel' these energetic shifts. Others will 'see' them. And, still others 'just know' what is happening energetically.

Unlike most social situations, people in Heart Circles can talk about what they are experiencing energetically within the Circle and receive 'reality checks' from others in any given moment. "The group feels a bit flat to me right now. Is that what the rest of you are feeling?"

Knowing how to deliberately read energy levels will allow you to be much more present and attuned to your inner and outer surroundings. If you can read them, energetic fields are more reliable indicators of what is actually happening in any given situation than listening to the words that people are speaking within that situation.

Again, the question is not what you 'think' about this; it is asking what you want in relationship to being more conscious of these energetic fields. Do you want to explore this together during your Heart Circle meeting?

Experiment: during the group, stop two or three times to ask how each person would describe the 'energy level' of the group at that particular moment. Does it feel high, low, edgy, calm, good, bad, dense, light, exciting, boring? Use your own words.

6. How much safety do you need from others to be more 'self-revealing' while in Circle? Do you want to take more risks with this?

Talking about things that you are 'afraid' to talk about in Heart Circle presents you with a paradox involving this kind of honesty. Being open with others requires a safe 'container' or environment in which to be open. However, the container becomes safer as people 'risk' being more honest when they don't necessarily feel safe in doing so.

In Heart Circles, this paradox is partially resolved by members agreeing that honesty is welcomed and honored. Every meeting brings with it opportunities for greater emotional honesty. Everyone can share what he or she honestly wants, feels, and thinks.

Sometimes it will be several months of meetings before your Heart Circle is strong enough to allow some member to reveal what he or she has never before shared. It is worth both the wait and the risk: secrets stop the flow of energy, and when those secrets are allowed to surface, they are normally replaced with joy.

It is important to remember, however, that it is not the purpose of Heart Circles to process deep emotional pain or to ferret out dark secrets. The purpose is to focus on what people truly want. But to be honest about what we want means we have to be honest about what we feel. For example, if someone wants better health, he or she will have to be honest about his or her current health status. If two people want a closer relationship, they will have to be honest about the distance between them at that point.

Experiment: consider being more open than you usually are concerning how you are feeling and what you are wanting and thinking during this Circle meeting. Watch or feel what happens to both you and the group when you do.

7. Are you clear about the differences between what you are thinking, feeling, intuiting, knowing and wanting? When people ask you what you are feeling do you tell them what you are thinking?

Heart Circles are laboratories to explore the differences between what you are thinking, feeling, intuiting, knowing, and wanting.

Experiment: focus on a topic that affects everyone in the room such as our 'global environment.' Start by asking everyone to offer 'one' belief that he or she has about this subject. Then have everyone share what he or she 'feels' about it, then have everyone say what he or she 'senses' or 'intuits' will happen in the future about it. Continue with what each person 'knows' about the environment and finally what each one 'wants' in relation to it. Answers need to be limited to just a few words or sentences per person.

For example:

'I *believe* what is happening in the environment is terrible.'

'I *feel* frustrated and sad about it.'

'I *sense* that things will get worse before they get better.'

'I *know* that we cannot ignore these issues, and expect them to go away.'

'I **want** to install solar panels on my roof at home.'

Clear communication is determined by people's ability to differentiate between these different terms. Most conflict between people comes from mixing them up. Some examples:

What I 'know' must be objectively verifiable while what I believe, by definition, can't be verified. If I confuse what I 'believe to be true' with what I 'know to be true,' I risk conflict with others who are similarly confused. We see this showing up in religious conflicts around the world.

If people ask me what I want and I tell them what I feel, the conversation goes nowhere. If they ask me what I'm feeling and I tell them what I think, they'll probably walk away confused.

Heart Circles provide an environment in which these kinds of distinctions can be made clearer.

8. Have you ever identified the different ways that one person in a highly functional group can derail it and make it dysfunctional?

Just as with an individual, the energetic level of a small group is continuously rising and falling, depending on what is happening within that group. Given this, be on the lookout for certain behavioral strategies that people use to lower the group's level when it becomes too high for their comfort level or if they have learned how to use the energy of the group to raise their own energetic level at the expense of the group.

There is no blame associated with using these strategies: no one is doing anything wrong when he or she uses them. At the same time, these strategies make any group difficult to be in when someone uses them unconsciously. To guard against this, these strategies need to be identified and changed:

Time Taking: consistently taking more time than others take while in Circle. Example: The Circle meets for two hours a week, and one person takes up half that time week after week.

Response holding: consistently holding back responses to whatever is happening in the group. Example: a member is hurt by what someone said in the group but says nothing about it.

Intellectualizing: consistently sharing thoughts, rather than what the individual wants or how he or she feels. Example: a member talks on and on, without coming to some point.

Story Telling: consistently focusing on events or the history of what has happened, rather than how those events affected that person and what that person wants as a result of those events. No example needed; we have all experienced this before.

Fixing: consistently offering 'solutions' in response to what others are sharing, rather than just listening compassionately. Example: someone says that he or she is sad, and someone else tells that person how to cheer up.

Bubble Bursting: consistently redirecting the focus of a group when it reaches a high level of intimacy or intensity. Example: everyone is having a profound moment of silence after something important is shared and someone cracks a joke to break the silence.

Dissonance: consistently going against what is happening in a group process by criticizing it, being oppositional, or playing confused. Example: someone saying, week after week, that there is something about what is happening within the group that he or she just does not like, but then never identifying what that is.

The purpose behind all of these behavioral strategies is to avoid intimacy and connection. Everyone will employ any one of these responses occasionally. When it becomes an ongoing pattern, your Circle will need to confront it compassionately and be clear about what others want in response to that pattern.

Experiment: talk about your personal experience with these strategies in other groups that you have been in.

9. Do you want to double your sense of humor? Practice, practice, practice!

High functioning Heart Circles move in and out of laughter. This happens spontaneously. If it isn't happening and your Heart Circle becomes very, very serious, consider laughing at that.

10. Do you want to become more grateful in life? If so, how would you go about that?

Some people say that the fastest way to joy is through gratitude.

Others speak of developing 'an attitude of gratitude' and that 'gratitude brings to us more of what we are grateful for.' Feeling grateful, itself, feels good.

Could it be that the desire to be more grateful is the key to being more grateful?

Experiment: see what happens to the energetic level of the group when each person takes a turn naming three things that he or she is truly grateful for in life.

11. When people share with you something important that they are going to do, how often do you call them up after they do it just to find out how it went? Do you want to do this more often?

As Heart Circle members share with each other what they are feeling and wanting during each meeting, follow-up opportunities arise. This kind of follow-up can happen both in between meetings and during subsequent meetings.

An example would be someone sharing that he or she has an important job interview during the week. A call to that person before or after the interview can be rewarding to both the caller and the called.

There will inevitably be ongoing projects or desires that each member shares, so receiving updates each meeting can bring a great sense of connection between members and offer continuity from one meeting to the next.

As with all other aspects of Heart Circle, however, this is not to be turned into a 'should' or into some prescribed ritual. Our heart intelligence will remember and act on matters important to it and to others without our needing to be 'strategic' about it.

Experiment: no need for one. Just do it, if you want to.

12. Have you experienced what it feels like to intentionally be aware of your physical heart area while you are talking with someone?

Holding our attention on our heart area activates heart intelligence.

If you want to know what you want, you will find out faster by feeling your heart area as you inquire.

If you want to feel gratitude, it is amplified when you hold your attention in your chest.

If you want to hear what people are actually saying, listen to them from your heart.

As you do this, you may experience how literal it is when we say a person is 'in his or her heart.'

Experiment: experiment with being aware of your heart area as many times as you can throughout the meeting. Share what you experienced at the end of the meeting.

13. When sitting in Heart Circle, is there physical contact (non-sexual) between you and the people sitting next to you: knees touching, hands held, etc.? Is this something that you are comfortable with or not? Do you all want to talk about it some time?

When we are with good friends in a nurturing environment, non-sexual physical contact can feel good. It can take us back to the days of childhood camaraderie when physical contact was spontaneous and natural.

Experiment: simply talk about this in Circle. Find out where everyone is in relation to this kind of intimacy. Then respect each person's boundaries in reference to this topic.

14. What if there was no such thing as a 'problem'? What if the worst problem in the world wasn't one?

One of the primary functions of 'thinking' is to solve problems. In our culture, in which we have been conditioned, trained, and rewarded to think about life constantly, rather than to feel it, life can be reduced to simply solving one problem after another.

Constantly solving problems becomes joyless rather quickly: push a problem up the hill; go down the hill to find another problem to push up the hill until there is just a continuous process of problem solving. Overachievers can become quite good at this. They become better problem solvers than others and are often financially rewarded for it.

But continuous problem solving is not only joyless, it also creates a perceptual reality in which life itself becomes a problem. This produces adrenal exhaustion, burnout, and a serious shortage of internal peace. Constant problem solving can be quite stimulating, but it can never serve as a basis for personal fulfillment.

Heart Circles create an environment to explore alternatives to problem solving. The process starts with the understanding that framing something as a 'problem' automatically activates a 'thinking' or mental response to it. The alternative is to:

- look factually at what is currently happening.

- witness what you are feeling about what is happening.
- find out what you want, given what is happening.

This question of 'what do I want' activates an entirely different part of the brain from what is used when we look at life problematically. Entertaining the question itself is inherently pleasurable. We will be energized, rather than energetically drained. We will also be far more creative because we will be more relaxed than when we are solving problems. Our thinking becomes clearer, and more possibilities open to us.

We can enter a 'no problem mode' whenever our desire to do so is stronger than our addiction to problem solving. Heart Circles help in this transition, for the focus is always on what each member wants, rather than on the problems that each member has.

Members will inevitably bring their personal problems to Heart Circle. This is to be encouraged. But, instead of fixing those problems with sound advice and excellent solutions, allow time for that problem to be articulated sufficiently, then go gently into the question, 'Given all this, what do you want?'

Do you have a problem with this?

15. One valuable aspect of Heart Circle is that it offers the opportunities to share information and resources with each other. Do you want your Heart Circle to include this kind of spontaneous sharing?

- a movie or book recommendation

- an upcoming event not to be missed

- an important news item to share

- a web site to check out, etc.

Because friends 'resonate' together, their sense of what is important and relevant to each other will likely resonate, as well. Exchanging information on films, books, web-sites, music, important news items, etc. provides another thread that will weave you together.

Experiment: so what movie have you seen lately that you want to recommend to your Circle? See what happens when you toss this question into the mix of things during this current meeting.

16. Have you ever had a 'best day in your life' because you intentionally wanted it to be that for you? Do you want to make this particular meeting the best Circle you have ever been in?

Experiment: this experiment has far reaching implications. As the Circle begins, find out if everyone is willing to make this meeting particularly enjoyable, as enjoyable or more so than any other. If all of the members agree that they want this, don't do anything special to make it so. Just stay in touch with wanting it to be enjoyable. At the end of the group, check in with the members as to whether or not they received the enjoyment that they wanted.

If your enjoyment was increased by this experiment, continue experimenting for the rest of your life.

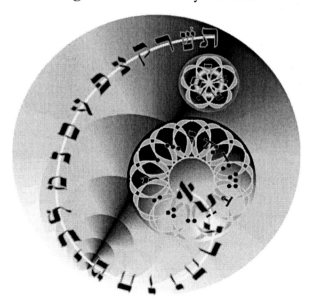

17. Do you want to listen so compassionately that you 'feel' what people are saying, rather than just hearing what they saying?

Billions and billions of dollars are spent annually in our culture advertising products and services to make us look better. Have you ever seen one commercial in your entire life for a product or service that helped you to listen better? (This does not include ads for hearing aids.)

Heart Circles are experiential gatherings in which to teach you how to listen to each other with greater empathy and compassion. The radio commercial for advertising this particular Heart Circle feature would sound something like this:

"Do your children come to you first when they have an issue they can't resolve? Are you known at work as someone who knows how to listen? Do you feel what people are saying or just think about what they are saying? Whether your answers to these questions are 'yes' or 'no,' Heart Circles guarantee that you will have the ultimate environment in which to learn how to listen with greater empathy and compassion. Heart Circles are free and self-forming, so call now at 1-800-LISTEN2 to find out more details. That's 1-800-LISTEN2."

18. Are you in touch with your capacity to 'choose' what you think and feel, rather than being 'stuck' with what you are thinking and feeling? Do you want to be more intentional about this?

Just by virtue of being alive, we are all continuously thinking and feeling. It comes with being human. And there is a developmental leap that occurs when an individual realizes that he or she has the capacity to 'watch' or 'witness' his or her own thoughts and feelings deliberately and consciously.

For those who have developed this capacity, a whole new world of opportunity opens up to them; they become aware that they have the freedom to begin choosing what they 'want' to think and what they 'want' to feel in any given moment. They slowly begin to find out that they can access which thoughts and feelings feel good to them and which feel bad. Then they get to 'choose' which thoughts and feelings they want to relate to as real or relevant to them.

The Heart Circle is one of the best classrooms available to practice this kind of artistry. Just as people can decide whether or not they want to do some particular thing, they can also decide, to a degree, how they want to think or feel.

For example, if someone thinks that he or she is not artistic, that individual can watch this thought flow through his or her consciousness and then decide to replace it with one that feels better: 'I may not draw well, but there are many areas of my life where I am artistic!'

Exercising the freedom to choose our thought and feeling states is one of the primary developmental tasks that we all face as human beings. John Lennon and Yoko Ono were referring to this freedom in the early Seventies when they created the infamous poster that read:

'War Is Over! (If you want it.)'

19. What is your intuitive sense of what will happen in the world during the next ten years? Could our civilization, as we know it change dramatically as it did for Europe in 1939 or for New Orleans in 2005? Is this something you want to talk about in Circle?

Most people don't want to talk about this in any circle. Some people even think that talking about it somehow contributes to it happening. Others feel overwhelmed by the subject and don't know where to begin talking about it. Still others refer back to the year 2000 and remember all the talk about the Y2K computer collapse.

What about you? Do you want to talk about this in your Heart Circle?

20. Are you good at recognizing all of the different realities around you or are you stuck in 'the' reality: your own? If you are stuck, do you want to get unstuck?

Heart Circles are unique in that they allow members to explore different realities or different energetic states. These different realities can include:

- physical realities

- emotional realities

- mental realities

- energetic realities

- spiritual realities

Knowing that there is such a thing as 'different realities' allows two seemingly contradictory ideas to both be true. For example, you can talk about an illness:

On a physical level, the reality may be that you have a viral infection and need antibiotics to counteract it. Every doctor would agree.

On a mental, emotional, and energetic level, the reality may be that the virus is simply a manifestation of what you are thinking and feeling. If you change those thoughts and feelings, you change the energetic environment so that it no longer supports that virus.

On a spiritual level, the reality may be that you are attracting an experience that you need in order to further expand your understanding.

Communication often breaks down when people are talking about the same thing, but from different levels of reality.

'I need antibiotics to get well.'

'No, you don't. You need to look at what you are thinking and feeling that is making you sick.'

'Now you're making me sick. Go away!'

Knowing that multiple alternative realities can all be true is an antidote for argument and war. You can explore this within your Heart Circle consciously.

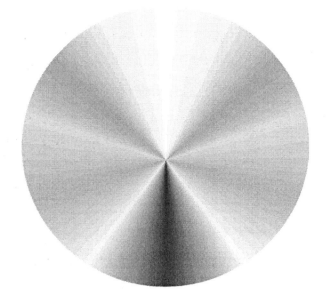

21. Do you know the difference between being present and being radiant? Are you aware of the male/female differences here?

A subject that comes up often in Heart Circles concerns 'relationships': issues between partners, the differences between masculine and feminine, wanting a mate, etc.

Teacher and author David Deida offers insight into this subject when he speaks of the 'deep masculine' and the 'deep feminine' and about how spirituality is rooted in these two essences. He says that it is by the man experiencing his own masculine nature and by the woman experiencing her feminine nature that harmony is created in a relationship.

He also speaks of there being three developmental stages of relationships:

The macho male and the Barbie Doll female stereotypically embody the first stage. This stage is ruled by dominance and submission.

The second stage relationship involves 'equality': the man becomes more sensitive and less domineering and the woman becomes more assertive and independent. This relationship is based on equality, mutual sharing, and genderless roles.

The third stage relationship sees the emergence of the deep masculine and deep feminine. The man becomes 'present' and the woman becomes 'radiant.' The man holds the focus and provides the direction in the relationship and the woman becomes the radiance and the inspiration for that direction.

Many relationship issues arise because the man isn't being 'present' and the woman isn't being 'radiant.'

We don't have to 'do' anything to be present or radiant; it is what we are. We do have to want to feel those two different essences in order to feel more embodied in them.

Experiment: the men in the Circle take three minutes to double their own sense of 'presence.' No instructions or explanations come with this: just 'double your presence.' At the end of three minutes, the women take three minutes to double their radiance. Again, no instructions or explanations are necessary. Then talk together about what you all experienced in those six minutes. Don't intellectualize this; talk about what you felt.

If you encounter any major obstacles with this process, call David Deida. He lives somewhere in Texas.

22. What do you want to do together, outside of the Circle this week?

People in Heart Circles have endless opportunities to extend their Circle friendships outside of Circle by doing things together and spending time with one another. There are also opportunities for group functions that arise from birthday or holiday celebrations, sporting events, camping trips, or service projects.

Experiment: get together with someone else in your Circle this week. Do whatever you want to do.

23. Does your Circle want to talk about 'sexuality' or is that a subject best left untouched (so to speak)?

In our culture, sex is used extensively to sell us stuff and to keep us entertained. Yet, there are few environments in which sexuality can be talked about openly and honestly. You may or may not want your Heart Circle to be such an environment, and you have the freedom to be open and honest about this. Again, it is your Circle.

24. Do you want to agree to show up for each other if someone in Circle is faced with a sudden personal crisis? Are you willing to call others in your Circle if that person in crisis is you?

There was a Heart Circle in the Detroit area in which one member was at the Detroit International Airport waiting for a flight and he was experiencing a serious emotional crisis. He didn't reach out to call anyone in his Heart Circle, even though that group had been together for six years. He managed to get through the crisis. When his Circle met, he reported what had happened to him. The other members asked why he had not called anyone from the Circle. He said that he had been ashamed of feeling so 'messed up.'

This led to a deep discussion and, from that, came an agreement that each member made with the others. If one person were to be in crisis, he or she had only to call the others in the Circle at any time, day or night, and use the key phrase, "I'm at the airport." This would signal everyone to drop everything and get to that person immediately, with no questions asked and no discussion. Four years later, that invitation is still intact with this group.

25. What do you need to transition from being in 'the' Circle to being in 'your' Circle? Are you comfortable with the responsibility that comes with it?

Own the Heart Circle that you are in. It is yours. The Circle is not complete without you. Don't agree to any changes in how the Circle functions, unless you want those changes. Take full responsibility for the energetic quality of what happens in Circle. If that quality declines for some reason, it's up to you to change that. It's your Circle. Don't 'shrink to fit' when you're in it. It's your Circle.

While doing this, honor the reality that it is everybody else's Circle, as well, and know that each member has the same ownership rights as you.

Wouldn't it be great if we all functioned in our families, schools, and businesses with this kind of fierce ownership, while, at the same time, not being at all possessive about it?

26. *What is your experience of 'surrender'?*

Have you ever been caught in a low energy state so that no matter what you do, you can't seem to move out of it? This can be a result of some devastating loss, or a pattern which you seem to be unable to break or simply a shadow part of you showing its fierce head with no regard whatsoever for how wise you have become.

One thing to do in this case involves 'sweet surrender.'. Do nothing. Forget everything written. Disregard all that you know. Simply sit in your pain and dysfunctional fear. Let it have you. Acknowledge that you have wrestled with a big bruising angel and got badly beaten. Be swallowed by the whale and give up all hope.

And within this black cavern of despair, let there remain only a tiny firefly flash of a question that arises on its own out of nowhere in the night. That question is a simple one: 'Given all this, what is it that I want?'

Then wait in silence for your answer to appear. That answer will come with patience and it will come from your heart. With it will also come an automatic reconnection to a higher energetic state because you have landed in your heart just by asking the question, and you are trusting that an answer will come.

But there are many ways to experience surrender. Create time for people in Circle to talk about what surrender means to them.

Heart Circle
Variations

Heart Circle Variations

There are several creative variations to the basic Heart Circle model that may serve you well.

Be Your Own Heart Circle:

You can receive value from reading this book even if you don't get involved with a Heart Circle. Meditate on what intrigues you as you read it. Use a personal journal to record your responses to the 26 questions. Explore the 'Law of Attraction' and advance your understanding of how to manifest what you want your life and world to be. Find out in all that is written here what is relevant and true for you. Use this manual as a reference tool.

Find A Focus Friend:

Much of what is described in this book can be explored with a friend. Commit to meeting weekly together for an hour. Follow the Heart Circle format. Decide on what agreements to keep with each other. Help each other to live more deliberately and joyfully.

Partnerships:

If you have a primary partner, the two of you can use the Heart Circle format to enrich your relationship tremendously. One of the primary reasons to be together can be your agreement to support each other in coming into greater joy by intentionally feeling what you want and opening yourselves to receiving it. Read this manual together to find out how you want to use the ideas contained within it.

Family Circles:

A family is a Heart Circle. You can set up informal family meetings weekly or bimonthly to find out what each person in the family is feeling and wanting. Children can directly participate from ages five and up. Encouraging them to communicate directly, giving them a sense of their being integral parts of the family regardless of their age, and treating them as beings who are participating in creating their own lives, rather than being victims to life can be just a few of the benefits to them of sitting in Circle together. Regular family heart circles increase family intimacy and bonding.

Creation Circles:

Creation Circles are for people who want to focus on specific creative interests or projects together. As with Heart Circles, they are self-forming and self-facilitated through consensual agreement.

Creation Circles may have two members or two hundred, depending on what the project or interest is. They may continue for months or years or fulfill their purpose in one meeting.

Creation Circles form because their members have a common interest and want to organize themselves to develop that interest. These different interests are virtually unlimited:

- *learning:* book clubs, workshops, lectures, study groups

- *the arts:* singing, acting, painting, dancing

- *mutual support:* grief, addiction, play, emotional processing

- *business:* investment, networking, sales, marketing

- *special events:* parties, memorial services, celebrations, festivals

- *recreation:* biking, camping, games, travel

- *hobbies:* collecting, gardening, building, chess

- *political action:* campaigning, education, fund raising, demonstrating

- *ecology:* cleanups, conservation, alternative energy, carpooling

- *health and healing:* meditation, yoga, jogging, massage

- *service:* food drives, mentoring, mediation, elderly care

- *relationships:* groups for couples, singles, gays, elders, teenagers

Creation Circles are designed to function according to the principles and practices of the Heart Circle. For example, in a Heart Circle, members are encouraged to first experience and then openly communicate what they 'want.' In a Creation Circle, when people have this same freedom to be honest about what they want, there is a huge increase in both efficiency and personal enjoyment. People are much more inclined to do what they say they are going to do when they really want to do it, rather than when they 'think' they should do it. This is good news for everyone but the volunteer martyr who is constantly saying 'Well, someone has to do it. I guess I will.'

Therefore, a central theme within Creation Circles is that people become involved in creative projects only when their hearts call them to do so. No one is asked to 'sacrifice' for the good of the organization or to do things out of a sense 'obligation.' Rather, people are simply encouraged to follow what feels 'good' to them; what feels 'right.'

There is a wonderful rabbi in Ashland, Oregon who, upon hearing this, renounced the entire idea of just following what one 'wants.' He said that this is egocentric and that true community itself is founded upon 'sacrifice' and 'service,' upon people emptying the bedpans of the sick and doing that which no one else wants to do. The rabbi himself modeled this by being an untiring and towering fountain of loving service in both his Jewish community and the community at large.

What the good rabbi didn't understand was that he loved what he was doing! He loved being of service! Emptying a bedpan was an act of worship to him. So there is no contradiction here! 'Service' from the heart feels magnificent! True 'sacrifice' is ecstatic. It is hardwired into us as humans, making it as blessed to give as to receive. Giving and receiving must be in balance for life to be in balance.

Men's or Women's Circles:

Something happens when men create Heart Circles with other men and women create Heart Circles with other women. There is a power inherent in this that other cultures and past civilizations understood and utilized. You may want to explore the idea of forming a gender specific group to find out for yourself what this means.

Heart Circles Within Existing Networks Or Organizations:

I believe that most organizations in the 21st century will organize themselves around some type of Heart Circle format. A church or temple, for example, can increase the creativity and self-organizing capacity of its individual congregants by tenfold almost overnight by encouraging small Heart Circles and Creation Circles development. It inverses the hierarchical structure of the organization so that the paid staff ends up doing 10% of what is accomplished while the members contribute the other 90%, instead of the other way around.

Heart Circles within Businesses:

It is common sense to say that when people within a business are allowed to work from the well of their passions, rather than from a position of just 'putting in time,' the business will flourish. With some modifications, Heart Circles within businesses can easily accomplish this.

Heart Circles within schools:

The inner life of children is completely 'left behind' in most schools today. Every child deserves to have a safe place within the school environment to express what he or she is feeling and wanting, to talk about relationships with classmates, and to learn how to follow his or her own heart. It would be relatively easy to organize Heart Circles in schools, if political support for doing so existed.

Heart Circles could also play a significant role on university and college campuses. These Circles provide ideal environments for students to experientially explore community building and their own inner wisdom, while they are, at the same time, involved in the academic world.

Phone or Internet Circles:

While it is obviously ideal to be in the physical presence of each other and living in the same town or city, Heart Circles can operate via teleconferencing calls or through the use of Instant-Messaging via the Internet. Again, just follow what is laid out in this Heart Circle manual, and enjoy.

Crop Circles:

Just kidding.

Sustainability Circles:

This is for those people wanting to combine the Heart Circle model with a direct focus on creating sustainable, local communities using the project-oriented Creation Circles. In order to move away from centralized monolithic

131

social structures, we must begin with small groups taking responsibility for change at a local level.

In Closing

In Closing

To intentionally come into Circle with friends and family has numerous benefits in relation to building sustainable communities. But community is not the ultimate purpose for being in Circle; it is the natural outcome. The ultimate purpose is for individuals to use the reflective and amplifying power of the Circle to better experience the relationship between what they focus on and what they attract.

As I write these closing comments for this book, I am aware that the focus of media outlets is on story after story of fear-laden news: war, terrorism, corruption, over-spending, and environmental stress. I am unwilling to 'switch' my focus away from these stories and pretend they are not real. But I want to keep my focus on them only long enough to allow what I 'see' to be an inspiration for me to feel and create what I 'want to see.' I want to feel and create more joy, more peace, more clarity, vision, creativity, courage, prosperity, play, and love. I want this in my own life and I want it in my world, both of which are intrinsically bound.

From these wants comes the question of how I want to use my passion and my gifts to manifest this. And my answer is that my passion and gifts lie in sharing with others how sitting in Circle provides a safe container in which to explore what their passions and gifts are in terms of manifesting the world which they want to see.

If this resonates with you, let's work and play together. I invite you to create your own Heart Circle and use it to amplify the callings of your heart. Let's do this together, not to form another monolithic, global organization, but to create thousands of gloriously unique, independent Heart Circles which are fully claimed and facilitated by the members within them. And let's talk to each other as we do this: from Heart Circle to Heart Circle.

I am grateful for the opportunity to share this Heart Circle book with you. And I am complete.

Tej Steiner

Appendix

Summary

Definition Of Heart Circles

Heart Circles provide ongoing small support group settings for people wanting to explore how to deliberately become more creative, joyful, focused, heart-directed, and responsive to the times in which they live. When people explore this together, they connect with each other spontaneously and quickly.

A new kind of community can emerge from this connection. The community holds space for individuals to live life from what they truly want instead of what they should or shouldn't do. Those individuals then offer back to the community the vitality and creativity of their passions and their clarity of purpose. This strengthens the community, which, in turn, creates an even more nurturing environment for the individuals within it. And on and on it goes.

Our species is at an evolutionary crossroads: we are moving out of a condition of operating on the basis of individual survival and collective competition into a new dynamic centered on individual happiness and collective cooperation.

There are certain insights or principles that we must understand and adhere to in order to move from suffering to joy.

The small support group format provides a perfect environment in which to explore these insights.

The purpose of this book is to show you how to create your own self-organized and self-facilitated Heart Circle.

Most of us had little personal support in deliberately creating happiness and connection as we have grown up and developed in our society.

Heart Circles work with principles or insights that provide a foundation for deliberately creating joy. Here are eight of those insights.

1. Everyone moves back and forth between happiness and unhappiness continuously, between feeling high and feeling low, between feeling good and feeling bad.

2. There is an unconscious or conscious desire in everyone to move out of pain and suffering and into happiness and joy.

3. There is a pivotal 'awakening' when we realize that we can actually choose to be in these higher energy states of joy, connection, and creativity.

4. The 'ultimate' practice for being in joy is to feel and then choose that which brings us joy. ('Joy' can be replaced with other words: peace, contentment, being in the moment, love, etc.)

5. There is a direct relationship between what we want and what we receive.

6. Feeling and following what we want requires that we distinguish between our 'hidden, conditioned wants' and our 'conscious, heart-felt wants.'

7. What we are manifesting in our lives that we don't want can be used to clarify what we do want.

8. In the 'higher' energetic states of love, joy, integrity, gratitude, etc. the actual experience of who we are changes dramatically. We go from thinking that we are separated from everything to experiencing that we are connected to everything.

Heart Circles are made up of people wanting to support each other in feeling and following what they love.

At this evolutionary crossroads in which we are moving from survival-based competition to 'thrival-based' cooperation, our survival may be dependent upon making this shift.

Heart Circles can be used to 'relocalize' our society.

There are five specific benefits of being in a Heart Circle.

1. Manifesting: In a Heart Circle, you have others who support you in manifesting joy in your life.

2. Friends: In a Heart Circle, you have friends who will celebrate with you the Process of Life.

3. In Crisis: In a Heart Circle, you have others who will be there for you, if crisis comes.

4. In Community: In a Heart Circle, you have others with whom to build sustainable communities.

5. In The Future: In a Heart Circle, you have others who'll be responding with you to the changes that are coming.

How to Create a Dynamic Heart Circle

Where To Start

Heart Circles are self-forming. They start with one or two people bringing several others together to experiment in terms of forming one. This book lays out the basic blueprint for the Heart Circle model.

Facilitation

Heart Circles are self-facilitated. The role of facilitator can be rotated so that at each meeting a different member facilitates or everyone can take responsibility for that facilitation process as the meeting unfolds.

Heart Circle Agreements

All relationships have spoken and unspoken agreements that the people in them require for the relationship to flourish. The following are agreements that experience has shown must be in place for a Heart Circle to flourish. However, these agreements cannot be imposed on anyone: they have to actually be discussed, and then agreement has to be reached by consensus.

Confidentiality: what happens and what is said in the Circle stays in the Circle. If this is violated, the Circle will not hold.

No third party talk: communication is direct between individual members, rather than triangulated with a third party.

Taking responsibility: speak only for yourself, instead of for others. Use 'I' statements rather than 'we' or 'you' statements. Reflect on how you have created any situation you are in, rather than being a victim of what that situation is.

Resolving conflict: if conflict arises between members, there is agreement to work it out directly and quickly, rather than letting any disagreement fester, unaddressed and hidden.

No drugs or alcohol: no smoking, drinking, or drug use during the 2 hour Heart Circle meeting.

Notification: if someone can't be at a meeting or will be late, there is an agreement to notify the group before the meeting begins.

Commitment: members pick a certain number of weeks during which they want to initially explore being in Heart Circle together. They then honor their agreement to show up for those weeks. Suggested initial time is 8 weeks.

Closure: if someone wants to leave the group before the initial eight weeks or afterwards, there is agreement to 'close' with the other group members *in person* during one of the Heart Circles, rather than through e-mail or by closing with members individually.

Consensus: any decision that the group makes about the group requires everyone's agreement.

Confrontation and Accountability: Heart Circles are *not* confrontational and are *not* about holding anyone accountable. The individual is accountable to him or herself only.

Staying within time boundaries: there is agreement to start Heart Circles on time and end on time. If anyone wants to change those times, it is done through consensus.

Heart Circle Suggestions

Meeting environment: The best place to hold a Heart Circle is in one of the member's homes, where there is comfort and privacy.

Food: In general, it is best to not meet and eat at the same time.

Privacy: Make sure that no one can overhear what is happening within your Circle while you are meeting, or that people walk into your meeting space once your Circle opens.

Heart Circle Format/ AGENDA

This 'agenda' is meant to be a flowing general guideline, rather than a formalized procedure set in stone. You don't need a stopwatch or a conversation cop, but you do need a sense of focused sensitivity to stay within the parameters outlined here. As the Heart Circle follows this format, over time, it can then eventually find its own rhythms and focus. As with life, the key to every Heart Circle meeting is the intention to enjoy being in it.

1. Tune-in: Heart Circle begins with everyone sitting in silence together, hands held, for 2 or 3 minutes. Clear your mind, get into present time, feel what you are feeling.

2. Check-in: each person takes 2 or 3 minutes to both inform the others as to how he or she is feeling as the Circle begins and to relay any significant event or insight that occurred since the previous Circle.

3. Discuss one of the Heart Circle Questions: there is a 20 minute group discussion on one of the 26 Heart Circle questions (below). This is designed to activate heart intelligence and increase group cohesion.

4. Explore what each member wants: each member takes from 10 to 15 minutes to talk about what he or she wants to manifest in one of the basic areas life: partnership or marriage, individual friends, community, work, money, play or leisure, health, learning or creativity, and the details of life (cleaning you're the house, picking up the laundry, etc.)

5. Back to the Heart Circle Question: there is a 10 minute discussion of how that meeting's Heart Circle question affected the Circle dynamic.

6. Closure: sit in silence together, hands held, followed by each member sharing a sentence on how he or she experienced the meeting or by naming one thing that he or she is grateful for as a result of being in the meeting.

The 26 Heart Circle Questions

These questions are unique. They come out of 20 years of small group facilitation experience, and have within them the power to draw out people's own inner wisdom and knowledge. They also are connective questions in that they elicit heart felt responses, rather than intellectualized opinions. And, even more magical, they lead to subtle observations of how small group dynamics actually work.

Use one question per Circle meeting for 26 meetings; then make up your own questions or use these over again. Enjoy!

1. What if we all agree to speak when we want to, rather than in some kind of linear order. Would we have chaos or would it lead to greater joy?

2. Have you been conditioned to withhold your positive responses from people, assuming that others don't want to hear them? Do you want to reverse this?

3. What's your experience in terms of being intuitive? What does it feel like when you are? In general, do you want to be more in touch with your intuition?

4. Have you ever explored your limit of how much happiness or intimacy you can take before you shut it off? When you are happy, do you wait for 'the other shoe to drop'?

5. What does it mean to be sensitive to the 'energetic dynamics' of the group you are in? Are you aware of your capacity to 'read the energetic level' of the group at any particular moment? Do you want to increase your sensitivity to these levels by talking with each other about them?

6. How much safety do you need from others to be more 'self-revealing'? Want to play with that a little bit by taking some risks?

7. Are you clear about the difference between your thoughts, your feelings, your intuitive 'knowing,' and your wants and needs? When someone asks you what you are feeling, do you tell him or her what you are thinking?

8. Have you ever studied the different ways that one person in a highly functional group can derail it and make it dysfunctional? Can you relate to the list of ways in which this can occur?

9. Do you want to double your sense of humor? Practice, practice, practice!

10. Do you want to become more grateful during the course of your life? If so, how would you go about doing that?

11. When people share with you something important that they are going to do, how often do you call them up after they do it just to find out how it went? Do you want to do this more often?

12. Have you ever played with intentionally being aware of your physical heart area while you are you are talking with someone? It is amazing!

13. When sitting in Heart Circle, is there any physical contact between you and the two people sitting next to you? Are you OK if there is or does it make you uncomfortable?

14. What if there was no such thing as a problem? What if the worst problem in the world wasn't one?

15. One valuable aspect of a Heart Circle is that it offers people opportunities to share information and resources with each other. Do you want your Heart Circle to include this kind of spontaneous sharing? (movies, books, news events, websites, upcoming events, etc.)

16. Have you ever had a 'best day in your life' or 'best vacation' because you intentionally wanted it to be that for you? Do you want to make this Heart Circle now, this particular meeting, the best Circle you have ever been in?

17. Do you want to listen so compassionately to others that you feel what people are saying, rather than just hearing what they saying?

18. Are you in touch with your capacity to 'choose' what you think and feel, rather than being 'stuck' with what you are thinking and feeling? Do you want to be more intentional about this?

19. What is your intuitive sense of what will happen in the world during the next ten years? Could our civilization, as we know it, change dramatically as it did for Europe in 1939 or for New Orleans in 2005? Is this something that you want to talk about in Circle?

20. Are you good at recognizing all of the different realities around you or are you stuck in 'your' reality as being the only reality? If you are stuck, do you want to get unstuck?

21. Do you know the difference between being present and being radiant? Are you aware of the male/female differences here?

22. What do you want to do together, with other members, outside of the Circle this week?

23. Does your Circle want to talk about 'sexuality' or is that a subject best left untouched (so to speak)?

24. Do you want to agree to show up for each other, if someone in Circle is confronted by a sudden personal crisis? Are you willing to call others in your Circle, if that person in crisis is you?

25. What do you need to transition from being in 'the' Circle to being in 'your' Circle? Are you comfortable with the responsibility that comes with it?

26. What is your experience in terms of 'surrender'?

HEART CIRCLE VARIATIONS

There are several creative variations to the basic Heart Circle model that may serve you well.

- Be Your Own Heart Circle

- Find A Focus Friend

- Partnerships

- Family Circles

- Creation Circles

- Men's or Women's Circles

- Heart Circles Within Existing Networks Or Organizations

- Heart Circles within Businesses

- Heart Circles within Schools

- Phone or Internet Circles

- Sustainability Circles

Heart Circle
Training Programs

Heart Circles are designed to be self-organized and self-facilitated. This means that you can gather with four or five other people you trust and simply begin meeting. There is enough basic information in this book to do this because your longing to form a Circle will activate your own inner heart guidance to assist you.

Heart Circles can also be transformative for existing organizations, churches, community networks, service clubs, or fraternal groups. They help people within such groups to connect with each other more deeply, while activating individual clarity and joy, thus enriching the effectiveness of the organization itself.

To assist both individuals and organizations I have created 'Heart Circle Trainings,' based here in Ashland, Oregon. It provides personal or organizational consulting, private coaching, and Heart Circle training workshops. If you have specific questions concerning your existing Heart Circle or want additional individual or organizational training in Heart Circle facilitation where you live, we are here to serve you.

To contact us for consultation and workshops visit our website: **www.HeartCircle.com**.

Or write to us at:

Heart Circle Trainings
PO Box 393
Talent, OR 97540
Email: Tej@heartcircle.com

Related Resources

Jerry and Esther Hicks are the source of the Abraham teachings and have been an important inspiration to me in writing this book.

They have hundreds of CDs and several books concerning 'Deliberate Creation.' They offer daylong seminars throughout the U.S., and I strongly recommend hooking up with the wisdom that flows through them. They can be reached through their web site: www.abraham-hicks.com. By mail, write to: Abraham-Hicks Publications, P.O. Box 960070, San Antonio, TX 78269.

Tom Atlee is a pioneer voice in articulating how we are witnessing our own evolutionary transition from competition to cooperation.

This is a man of spiritual reason. His latest book is The Tao of Democracy. His website is: www.co-intelligence.org. By mail: The Co-Intelligence Institute, P.O. Box 493, Eugene, OR 97440.

Sam Harris boldly addresses the issue of how moderate religion inadvertently supports religious fundamentalism in his book, *The End of Faith*.

He challenges our most basic assumptions about organized religion, while, at the same time, being spiritually uplifting. His website is www.samharris.com.

Richard Heinberg's book, *Power Down*, provides 'options and actions for a post-carbon world.'

It is a sobering read, and well worth the time, if you are feeling hung over from the cheap-oil party which we have been attending for the last 100 years. His website is www.museletter.com.

Neale Donald Walsh has sold over 10 million books in his *Conversations with God* series. In all of his books, he demonstrates how life can change when we open up dialogue with our highest inner frequencies.

While most people reading this book are familiar with his work, they may not be aware of the ReCreation Foundation which he has established to advance conscious living. It is doing good work. The website is www.cwg.org.

The Mankind Project offers a male initiatory weekend that has been attended by over 30,000 men from around the world.

These weekends provide men with powerful opportunities to get in touch with both their life missions and their heart connections with other men. Their website is www.mkp.org. One of the co-founders, Bill Kauth, has written the best 'how-to' guide available for organizing men's support groups, entitled, *A Circle of Men*. His website is: www.sacredlifeboats.com.

Shaktari Belew's, *Honoring All Life* is an amazing resource book on building community and new paradigm perceptions.

'It is a comprehensive reference guide to those who offer creative solutions to humanity's most pressing environmental, cultural, and political issues.' Her website is: www.honoringalllife.org.

I have a personal fascination with essential oils and have used them extensively during the entire time that I was writing this book. (clary sage and lavender)

They directly affect the expansion of our energetic bodies, and I recommend that you experiment with using them. Visit www.essentialthree.com.

Andre is the artist who created the amazing mandalas found in this book.

His work is dedicated to the wellness and uplifting of life; his art is offered in the spirit of love, joy, and abundance for all. If you like the mandalas in this book, see them in full color on his website: www.livinglightcreations.com. His art is transformative. Enjoy.

Acknowledgements

This book carries the energies of several thousand people with whom I have sat in Circle during the past 20 years. I am so grateful for the privilege of being a Heart Circle pioneer with you.

In Detroit: Thank you to the group that supported me as I found my way from facilitator to full participant: Joe Maiorano, Bob Gothro, Bart Bauer, Mike Birskey, Greg Meenahan, and David Smith. The Canadian wilderness canoe trips that went along with our meetings have been highlights of my life.

Also, thanks to all the others in the Detroit Circles, with special thanks to lifetime brothers Dave Cobb and Bernie Ahearn.

In Ashland: The three groups that have helped me find out just how unique each Heart Circle is. Thanks to the 'therapists' group where we are heart therapists for each other: Glenda Feinsmith, Susan Wrona, and Lenn Snyder. The 'experimental' group in which we explore Heart Intelligence: Kirsten Liegemann, Shaktari Belew,

Jhoti Rundel, Tom Stekkinger, Carlo Kashanre, and Karen Kiester. And the outrageously powerful 'Relentless Optimists' in which we have helped each other to birth our 'social inventions': Bill Kauth, Craig Comstock, Lenn Snyder, Ron Kurtz, and Jeff Golden.

In Sebastopol: Special thanks to Shyama, Elizabeth, Jahn, and Jeff for all of the love and support and pure enjoyment that was part of doing this work there with you.

In Cleveland: Thank you to all of the 'Men In Circle' during the past eight years. Special thanks to you, Paul and Lynn Lubben for hosting, holding space , and being wonderful friends.

In Tulsa: Thank you, Karen and John Thomas and Terry and Catherine Padgett!

In Austin: My thanks to you, Ron and Lenore Scott at Unity Hills Church.

Back here in Ashland, Oregon where so many visionaries have gathered to find out why we are all here together, I want to thank the Conversations With God Foundation for all of the support that we received in terms of helping you to establish Heart Circles within your inspired network: Rachael Kennedy, thank you for understanding as deeply as you do what this is all about, as well as to you, Joanna Gabriel and Neale Donald Walsh.

Also, Kirsten Liegmann and Dominic Allamano: what a privilege to work with you so closely on 'In My Village.' We are just beginning.

As for the inspirational and technical support of this book, I so appreciate your professional editing input Craig Comstock, and also your critical input, Lenn Snyder, Marc Grail, and especially you, Caryn.

Bart and Pat Bauer and my mother, Sue Steiner, your contributions afforded me the initial time to begin this book.

Thanks to Grant Plowman and Linda Nichols at Interactive Media Publishing for your creative input and comprehensive business approach. You are an amazing resource!

To mentors who have been particularly inspiring to me, thank you, Ross Laing, Esther and Jerry Hicks and George Pransky. And, to my two closest mentor friends, Bill Kauth and Lenn Snyder, thank you.

And then, there is the family Heart Circle I live in: my wife, Caryn, my son, Amrit and his partner Susan who are the parents of my granddaughter, Vayla Rose; also Andrew, Staci, and Lissy, as well as the Bernards, Jason, and my daughter, Pritham. Thank you!

About the Author

Tej Steiner has been an independent facilitator of small support groups for the past twenty years. He was the founder of 'Men in Circle' that trained men to create their own men's groups. He is also the co-creator of 'In My Village,' an innovative community sustainability project that uses Heart Circles to 're-localize' communities. He is currently the founding director of 'Heart Circle Trainings.'

He has a passionate interest in creating new social structures that awaken the vision, joy, and creativity of the individual and is a lifetime student of politics, history, and consciousness transformation. He is a sculptor and the author of *Help Your Inner Artist Out: 20 Enjoyable Exercises*.

He lives in beautiful Ashland, Oregon.